Puritans, Pilgrims, and Merchants

Puritans, Pilgrims, and Merchants

Founders of the Northeastern Colonies

Kieran Doherty

The Oliver Press, Inc.
Minneapolis

*Page 2: **William Penn sails for the New World on the** Welcome.*

The Oliver Press, Inc.
Charlotte Square
5707 West 36th Street
Minneapolis, MN 55416-2510

For Mary Doherty, my mother, who taught me to love books and reading.

Library of Congress Cataloging-in-Publication Data
Doherty, Kieran.
Puritans, pilgrims, and merchants: founders of the northeastern colonies / Kieran Doherty.
    p.   cm.—(Shaping America)
Includes bibliographical references and index.
    Summary: Discusses the lives of eight people who were responsible for the founding of colo-
nial settlements from Massachusetts to Pennsylvania.
ISBN 1-881508-50-1 (library binding)
1. Atlantic States—Biography—Juvenile literature. 2. Atlantic States—History—Juvenile
literature. 3. United States—History—Colonial period, ca. 1600-1775—Biography—Juvenile
literature. [1. Atlantic States—History. 2. United States—History—Colonial period,
ca. 1600-1775. 3. Colonists—Atlantic States.] I. Title. II. Series.
F106.D64   1999
974—DC21
[B]   98-10957
                                        CIP
                                        AC
ISBN 1-881508-50-1
Printed in the United States of America
05 04 03 02 01 00   8 7 6 5 4 3 2

Contents

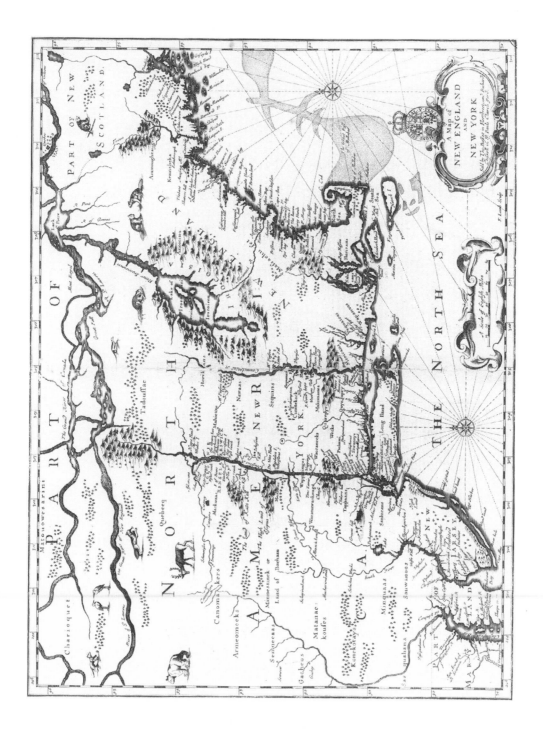

6

Introduction

More than 30,000 years ago, the first immigrants made their way to the North American continent. Drawn by huge, rich hunting grounds, these hunters crossed the Bering Strait from Siberia to far western Alaska on what is called the Bering Land Bridge, a dry causeway that then joined North America and Asia.

Over a period of thousands of years, the descendants of these northern Asian hunters and of later waves of migrants traveled to the south and east until they peopled the Americas from northern Canada all the way to the cliffs of Patagonia in South America. As these groups spread, they developed different ways of living. Some migrated to what is now the southwestern United States and eventually became cliff-dwelling peoples. Others made their way to the Great Plains between the Mississippi River and the Rocky Mountains, where they grew corn and hunted buffalo. Some voyaged, probably in dugout canoes, to the Caribbean Islands. Over the course of centuries, many others migrated to what is now the northeastern United States.

North America in 1676, after little more than a half century of European settlement

7

The Pequots, Wampanoags, Narragansetts, and other peoples of northeastern North America were members of the Algonquian-speaking family of tribes. They were mostly peaceful people, although there were wars between tribes for hunting grounds. Another major group was the more warlike Iroquois, who lived in southern Canada and in what became New York. Until the 1500s, these Native Americans—descendants of the true "first comers"—were the only humans in the northeastern regions of America. Then came the Europeans.

The English and Dutch people who settled the northeastern area were not the first Europeans to establish colonies in America. The Spanish had founded permanent settlements in Florida and New Mexico in the mid-sixteenth century. Soon after that, the English attempted to establish a settlement on Roanoke Island in what is now North Carolina. Although that attempt failed, by 1607 the English had established a permanent presence in the New World at Jamestown in Virginia.

The years following the founding of Jamestown saw the beginning of rapid settlement all along the Atlantic Coast. The settlers who braved the Atlantic Ocean and the unknown dangers of the wilderness in the northeastern frontier came for a variety of reasons. Some sought religious freedom, while others came in search of freedom from want. A few were fortune hunters. To all, however, the New World offered opportunity.

In this book, we will look at the settlement of the territory that stretched along the Atlantic

While Christopher Columbus (1451-1506) is called the "discoverer" of America, his voyage of 1492 was not the first to reach the shores of the New World. There is solid evidence that the Vikings landed in Newfoundland 500 years before Columbus. And it is likely that Middle Eastern adventurers from Phoenicia reached Central America about 1,000 years before the Vikings. In the century following Columbus's voyage, a number of explorers visited the New World, fueling Europeans' desire to settle in America.

The English claims to North America were based on the explorations of John Cabot and his son Sebastian in 1497 and 1498. This fanciful drawing—complete with polar bears—shows the two men landing on the island of Newfoundland off the east coast of Canada.

seaboard from the Canadian border on the north to the Delaware River on the south. That territory included what are now the states of Pennsylvania, New Jersey, New York, Connecticut, Massachusetts, Rhode Island, New Hampshire, Vermont, and Maine. The story of the founding of colonies in those states encompasses more than 150 years of America's early history, from the early 1600s to the Revolutionary War in the 1770s.

This book tells the stories of seven men and one woman who founded important settlements. These are tales of adventure and heroism, suffering and success—and they are true. A Dutchman, Peter Stuyvesant, ruled as director-general of what is now New York for his profit-hungry employers, the

The first permanent European settlement in North America was Saint Augustine, Florida, established by the Spanish in 1565. Plymouth in present-day Massachusetts was the first settlement on the northeastern frontier. It was founded in 1620 by a group of people we call Pilgrims.

Dutch West India Company. Englishman William Penn, in contrast, gave up a life of ease to follow his conscience. The founder of Pennsylvania and its first great city, Philadelphia, Penn established a form of government that Thomas Jefferson used as a model for the Declaration of Independence.

Like Penn, most founders sought to create a new society that better fit their ideals. As leader of the Pilgrims, William Bradford guided the early success of New England's Plymouth Colony. John Winthrop and the Puritans fled English persecution to found the nearby Massachusetts Bay Colony.

Though victims of intolerance in England, many of the Puritan leaders in the Bay Colony, including John Winthrop, also repressed other religious beliefs. Disputes over religion forced some to leave the Bay Colony and establish other settlements along the Atlantic Coast. The intolerance of the early Puritans accelerated the pace of settlement of America's northeastern frontier.

In this book you will read about several people who were banished from the Massachusetts Bay Colony. Fleeing arrest, Roger Williams built the first settlement in Rhode Island. Williams's aid was crucial in helping another religious rebel, Anne Hutchinson, found a second town in Rhode Island. John Wheelwright settled Exeter, New Hampshire. Distressed by all the contention in the Bay Colony, respected minister Thomas Hooker and his loyal parishioners founded the town of Hartford, Connecticut. Refusing to bow to authority, these upstarts opened up the northeastern frontier.

"Who can desire more content[ment] than to tread, and plant that ground he hath purchased by the hazard of his life? . . . What to such a mind can be more pleasant, than planting and building a foundation for his posterity, got from the rude earth, by God's blessing and his own industry?"
—John Smith, describing New England

Today it may be difficult to understand why religion or a desire for wealth would drive people to move across a broad ocean to live in hovels with an unsure supply of food. And we should not forget that their success caused immeasurable devastation to the peoples who already lived on the continent of North America. But we can admire the courage it must have taken these founders to leave home and friends—indeed, all that was familiar—for the dream of a better future.

This British military map of the English colonies in North America shows how much of the land was settled in 1766, a decade before the American Revolution. Louisiana and New Mexico were Spanish territories at that time. Notice the large area designated as "Lands Reserved for the Indians."

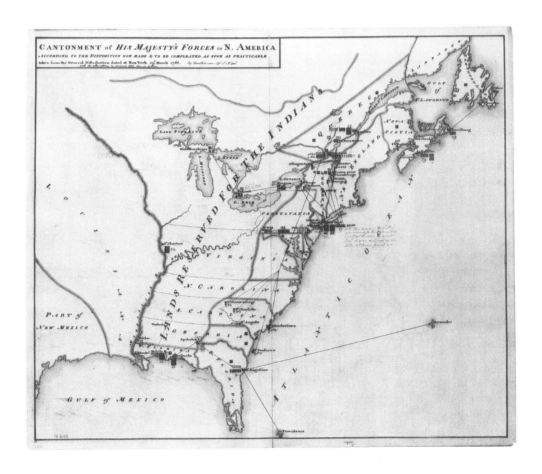

Chapter One

William Bradford
and the
Pilgrims of Plymouth

I n September of 1620, a tiny ship set sail from England bound for the New World of America. The *Mayflower* was about as long as a modern-day basketball court but only half as wide. On that voyage, it was crowded with 102 passengers, including 42 men, women, and children we have come to know as the Pilgrims. One those Pilgrims was 30-year-old William Bradford. Although we can be sure no one on board the *Mayflower* knew it at the time, Bradford was destined to become one of the most remarkable of America's founders.

William Bradford was born in March 1590 in the farming village of Austerfield in northern England. After the death of his father when he was only one year old, Will was shuttled from family member to family member until he ended up with

The Mayflower, *the Pilgrims' famous ship. We call the Plymouth settlers Pilgrims because, like people who go on pilgrimages, they traveled to the New World for religious reasons. They were not, however, generally known by that term until the middle of the nineteenth century.*

England's King Henry VIII (1491-1547) did not stop at one wife. After divorcing Catherine of Aragon, he went on to marry and divorce—or execute—four more women before settling on Catherine Parr, his sixth wife, who outlived him.

his uncles Robert and Thomas. Because of the turmoil he had endured in his young life, Will placed his hopes in God when he was just a boy.

In those years, England was in the midst of a religious revolution that had begun more than 50 years earlier. King Henry VIII had founded the Anglican Church in 1536 after the Roman Catholic pope refused to grant him permission to divorce. After that, Anglicanism became the official religion of England. For this reason, the Anglican Church was also called the Church of England. Some Anglicans thought their church was still too similar to the Catholic Church. Because they wanted to "purify" their church of all traces of Catholicism, they became known as Puritans.

Some people feared the church would never change, so they left the Church of England to form their own churches. These men and women were known as Separatists because they separated from the Anglican Church instead of trying to change it. At the time Will was growing up in Austerfield, Separatists in England were being arrested and often jailed for daring to leave the official church.

Drawn to their religious devotion, Will began attending Puritan services near Austerfield when he was about 12 years old. A couple years later, the teenager joined a Puritan congregation in the town of Scrooby near his home. The Scrooby congregation soon separated itself from the Anglican Church. Worn down by persecution in England, 18-year-old Bradford and the other Separatists of the Scrooby congregation fled in 1608 and eventually found refuge in Leiden, Holland, where persecution on religious grounds was against the law.

Although the Scrooby Separatists were free to worship as they pleased in Holland, they were unhappy living in a foreign culture. After about a decade, they decided to settle in the New World. There they hoped to establish a colony where they could live as English people but remain separate from the world and free from religious persecution.

Following several years of negotiations with the Plymouth Company—the joint-stock company that held the charter to settle New England—the Separatists obtained permission to go to the New World. They also had to search for ways to pay for their move since the Plymouth Company collapsed and later had to be reorganized as the Council for New England. They finally received financial backing from Thomas Weston, a London merchant, who formed another joint-stock company with a group of tightfisted London investors.

By this time Bradford was one of the leaders of the Scrooby group. It is believed he was one of the Separatists who was in charge of raising money for the voyage and dealing with the London investors.

On July 31, 1620, Bradford and about 50 other Separatists left for England. His wife, Dorothy, an English Separatist he had married in Leiden in 1613, also came, but they left their 5-year-old son, John, in Amsterdam, probably with Dorothy's parents. John did not come to America until he was 11 years old.

In Southampton, Bradford and the others were pleased to find the *Mayflower* ready to cross the

Joint-stock companies, which financed most of the early settlements in the Northeast, sold shares to investors and used the money raised to purchase ships, building materials, livestock, and all the other supplies needed to start a settlement. In return for their investment, stockholders expected to earn a profit, usually on furs and crops that would be shipped from the New World back to England.

July 31 was the date according to the Old-Style calendar the Pilgrims used. Using our calendar, the date would be 10 days later.

ocean. But they had unexpected companions for their journey. Weston had recruited about 60 non-Separatists as settlers. The Separatists referred to them as "Strangers" while calling themselves "Saints" because they believed they were saved.

On September 6, 1620, the *Mayflower* put to sea. The two-month ocean passage was brutal. The passengers spent long days and nights huddled below deck as the ship was battered by gales. Just two people—a crew member and a servant—died, a small number for those days. "After long beating at sea," Bradford wrote later, "they fell with that land which is called Cape Cod; . . . they were not a little joyful."

The Pilgrims had originally intended to settle near the mouth of the Hudson River, where New York City is now located. Instead, they decided to remain in Cape Cod in what is now Massachusetts. No one knows exactly why they stopped there, but some historians think pressure from the Strangers forced the Pilgrims to land before reaching the Hudson.

As the ship lay at anchor, some of the Strangers threatened to establish their own rule on land. The Pilgrims were outnumbered, but Bradford and the other Pilgrim leaders managed to convince almost all the men on board to sign a document known as the Mayflower Compact. The Mayflower Compact created the first English democracy, giving the men who signed the compact the right to vote and to establish laws. As soon as the compact was signed, the new citizens elected a Separatist named John Carver to be the colony's first governor.

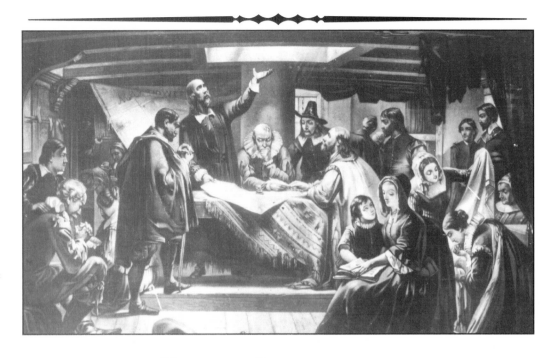

The Mayflower Compact

In the Name of God, Amen. We whose names are underwritten, the loyal subjects of our dread sovereign Lord King James, by the Grace of God of Great Britain, France, and Ireland King, Defender of the Faith, etc. Having undertaken, for the Glory of God and advancement of the Christian Faith and Honour of our King and Country, a Voyage to plant the First Colony in the Northern Parts of Virginia, do by these presents solemnly and mutually in the presence of God and one of another, Covenant and Combine ourselves together into a Civil Body Politic, for our better ordering and preservation and furtherance of the ends aforesaid; and by virtue hereof to enact, constitute and frame such just and equal Laws, Ordinances, Acts, Constitutions, and Offices, from time to time, as shall be thought most meet and convenient for the general good of the Colony, unto which we promise all due submission and obedience. In witness whereof we have hereunder subscribed our names at Cape Cod, the 11th of November, in the year of the reign of our Sovereign Lord King James, of England, France and Ireland. . . . Anno Domini 1620.

The "diverse cornfields" had been planted by the Wampanoags. Their village, Patuxet, had been wiped out by smallpox transmitted to the Indians by European fishermen who netted fish on North American shores for decades before permanent settlement. This drawing of Patuxet was made by explorer Samuel de Champlain before the epidemic of 1617.

After several weeks of searching for a place to build their settlement, Bradford, Carver and other men in the company rowed ashore at the site of what is now Plymouth. There, on December 11, they found "diverse cornfields and little running brooks, a place (as they supposed) fit for situation," recalled Bradford. Pleased with the spot they'd found—an abandoned Indian village, as it turned out—Bradford and the others returned to the *Mayflower*.

Any joy Bradford felt at choosing the site of the new settlement was surely crushed when he returned to the ship. His young wife, Dorothy, had somehow fallen overboard and drowned.

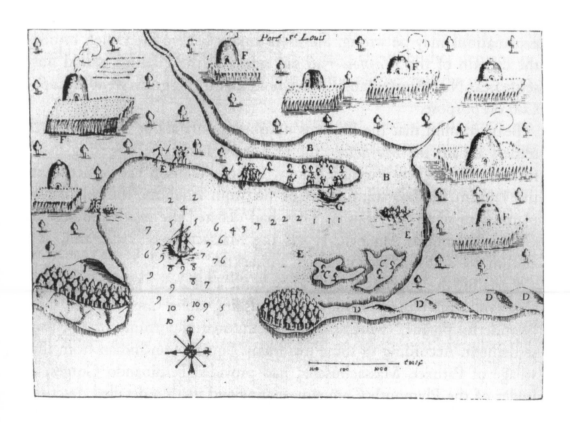

Massachusetts before the Pilgrims

Long before the first European set eyes on the territory that became the state of Massachusetts, the region was densely populated. The lands were home to a number of Algonquian-speaking Native American tribes, including the Wampanoags, the Nausets, and the Massachusets, after whom the colony of Massachusetts was named.

The Algonquian-speaking peoples of the Northeast lived in oval-shaped lodges in settled villages. In addition to hunting and fishing, they farmed corn, beans, and squash. The Indians worshipped a creator god, and they believed that humans and all other living things had immortal souls. Their spiritual leaders sought to bring them success in hunting or farming by convincing the souls of animals and plants to be generous to them.

The Massachuset Indians lived in a dozen or more confederated villages along the coast between Plymouth and Salem, Massachusetts. The Wampanoags controlled the region around Plymouth and further to the south, including the area of Cape Cod, where the Nauset Indians lived under their domination.

It is thought the first European to see Massachusetts was the Italian-born navigator and explorer Giovanni da Verrazano, who sailed along the coast of what we know as New England in 1524. For many years after Verrazano's visit, the only Europeans to visit were fishermen who came to the coast to fill their nets.

In 1602, Englishman Bartholomew Gosnold reached the shores of present-day Massachusetts and named such places as Cape Cod and Martha's Vineyard. Building on Gosnold's sightings, Captain John Smith explored much of the coastline between Virginia and Canada after arriving on the eastern seaboard in 1614. Smith (who also founded the Jamestown settlement in Virginia) fell in love with the region he called New England. In the years following his exploration, he wrote two books promoting the region and urging its settlement—*A Description of New England* and *Advertisements for the Unexperienced Planters of New England, or Anywhere*. His writings attracted a great deal of attention in England.

By the time the colonists began to arrive, the American Indian population in New England had been severely reduced. English fishermen had brought smallpox to the New World, which proved deadly to the natives, who lacked any natural immunity to the disease.

The Plymouth settlers' rural backgrounds were a great help when putting up their new homes in the wilderness.

Despite his grief over his wife's death, Bradford had to help found a colony. The *Mayflower* set sail for Plymouth harbor but anchored about a mile from land because the water was so shallow. The first settlers rowed a boat to the shore and stepped onto the land that was to be their new home. On Christmas Day, they began building their settlement. They didn't mind working on Christmas since they did not believe in celebrating that holiday.

Soon, small log houses were erected and a street was laid out from the waterfront to the top of a nearby hill. But tragedy continued to loom over the Plymouth settlers. They had nothing to eat but salt meat, dried peas, and hard biscuits. Almost all

were sick with fever and scurvy, a life-threatening illness caused by malnutrition. By mid-March, only about half of the villagers were still alive.

In the midst of these trials, a lone Indian walked into the settlement and spoke to the settlers in broken English. The man was Samoset, an Algonquin Indian who was visiting the nearby Wampanoag tribe. Samoset spent the night in the settlement before departing to meet his friends. He returned a few days later with Massasoit, the Wampanoag chief, and about 60 warriors. One of those men was Squanto.

Squanto was the sole survivor of the villagers who had been living on the site of Plymouth before smallpox wiped them out. He had been kidnapped by a British slave trader who had raided the coast near Cape Cod. As his fellow villagers were dying, Squanto was escaping slavery in Europe and trying to find a way back home. Since he had learned English during his captivity, he immediately became Plymouth's translator. Squanto, Bradford said, was "a special instrument sent of God for their good beyond their expectation." Indeed, the Pilgrims might not have survived had it not been for help from Squanto and the other Indians.

With Squanto's aid, life in the colony slowly improved, at least for a time. Massasoit and the Pilgrims had signed a treaty in which they pledged to defend each other if either was attacked by another Indian tribe. Just as critical to survival, Squanto showed the Pilgrims how to plant corn and use small fish for fertilizer.

"It pleased God to visit us then with death daily, and with so general a disease that the living were scarce able to bury the dead, and the well not in any measure sufficient to tend the sick."
—William Bradford to Thomas Weston, 1621

Because it was a New World crop, what we have come to call corn was unknown to the British. "Corn" and "wheat" are both general British terms for grain. That a vegetable acquired the name corn indicates how important it was to the settlers' diet.

Thanks to the peace treaty with Wampanoag chief Massasoit (c.1580-1661), the Pilgrims mostly lived in peace with the neighboring Indians for half a century.

When the captain of the *Mayflower* prepared to sail back to England in early April, not one of the Pilgrims asked to go home. But the dying had not ended. Later that month, Governor John Carver left the fields in the midst of the planting, complaining that he was ill. Within three days, he was dead.

After Carver's death, 31-year-old Bradford was elected governor. He would be reelected to the one-year position 30 times in the next 36 years. As the governor of the colony, Bradford was in charge of its day-to-day operations. During the colony's early years, his main concern was survival, but he also tried continually to gain a royal charter for the colony. That document would protect the holdings granted in 1621 to Plymouth by the Council for New England, the English joint-stock company that held the charter for New England.

In the autumn of 1621, the settlers began harvesting their crops and Plymouth finally appeared to be on a firm foundation. The Pilgrims, wrote Bradford, "had all things in good plenty." It was probably in mid-October that Bradford and the Pilgrims hosted the famous first Thanksgiving to give thanks to God for their survival. Massasoit and 90 other Wampanoags were their guests. But the cooking fires had barely cooled when about 35 young men arrived from England. Bradford complained that these new colonists, sent by the investor Thomas Weston, brought with them "not so much as a biscuit-cake or any other victuals."

Weston kept sending more settlers without provisions even as he demanded a return for his investment in the new colony. Each new boatload of newcomers caused further shortages of food and lodging. Time after time, when the settlement seemed to be on the verge of disaster, luck—or what Bradford called God's "Providence"—saved the day.

Although Providence may have had a hand in saving the colony, Governor William Bradford was Plymouth's real salvation. On one occasion in the spring of 1622, when "famine began now to pinch them sore," the governor learned that an English fishing fleet was nearby. He immediately sent several colonists to the boats to get supplies and then carefully rationed the food to make sure it would last until the crops were ready to harvest.

Later that same year, the colony lost one of its greatest helpers when Squanto died of what Bradford called "Indian fever." He became ill when he and Bradford were on a voyage to trade beads and knives for corn. According to Bradford, when Squanto was dying, he asked the governor to pray that he might go to the Englishmen's heaven. Bradford remembered Squanto's death as "a great loss."

More trouble hit the colony in March 1623. When Bradford heard that Massasoit was gravely ill, he immediately sent Edward Winslow, one of the colony's leaders, to help the chief. Luckily, the illness was only a digestive problem, and the medicine that Winslow brought cured Massasoit. The grateful chief warned Winslow that some of the other Indian tribes were planning to attack the nearby settlement of Wessagusset. If they were victorious, they would then wage war on Plymouth.

Edward Winslow (1595-1655) was already acquainted with Massasoit from their peace treaty negotiations. He served as Bradford's assistant for many of his years in office. This portrait is the only known painting of a Pilgrim.

Wessagusset, which was located about 25 miles from Plymouth, had been founded by another group of settlers sent from England by Weston. Soon after building their lodgings, these newcomers began stealing corn from the Indians. While Bradford had little sympathy for the thieves, he knew the Indians must be stopped or they would also destroy Plymouth. He dispatched Miles Standish, who was in charge of Plymouth's defenses, and eight other armed men to Wessagusset. Standish and his men trapped three Indian warriors and stabbed them to death. A fourth was captured and hanged. As word of the swift action spread, the threat to Plymouth died.

In spite of Plymouth's struggle for survival, Governor Bradford soon felt confident enough in the colony's future to welcome another newcomer. Alice Southworth, the widow of a Separatist, came to Plymouth from Leiden with her two sons. In August 1623, just a few weeks after her arrival, she and Bradford married. William and Alice Bradford would have three children together, a daughter and two sons.

Under Bradford's leadership, Plymouth grew and prospered. By mid-1622, an eight-foot wall surrounded the town and homes built of hewn logs lined the town's main street. Cattle and other livestock were brought from England and wild turkeys were domesticated. The Pilgrims could even start giving Weston a little money, for Hobomok, another Wampanoag, had helped them establish fur-trading networks with neighboring Indian tribes.

The Pilgrims' log homes were thatch roofed and covered on the inside with cedar shingles. One big room with a fireplace made up the ground floor. Above that room was a loft, reached by a ladder, where the children usually slept.

Although the colony began to thrive, it was unable to return a profit for Weston's partners. Some of the investors began withholding their financial support. Bradford knew that Plymouth could not become successful so long as the colonists were working for Weston's company and not for themselves. In 1627, he and seven other Pilgrim leaders made arrangements to pay off the debt owed to their financial backers. In exchange, the investors gave up their claims to property and trading rights in the colony.

Once they had gained control of the colony's resources, Bradford and the other leaders distributed all commonly owned land and livestock among the heads of family and single men in the colony. By giving settlers their own plots of land in the settlement, Bradford did much to assure Plymouth's future. The governor further strengthened the colony in 1630 by obtaining another charter from the Council for New England. Ten years later, he and the other proprietors who held that charter turned their claim over to Plymouth's settlers. The body of laws that the colonists created in 1636 showed they were confident that their colony was there to stay.

By 1630, just 10 years after the Pilgrims first landed in the New World, Plymouth was a fortified village of some 300 residents. The English population in the area would soon multiply because the religious persecution of Puritans in England was worsening. Like the Pilgrims, they, too, fled to the New World. Suddenly, in about a year's time, 2,000

The Separatists left England because they felt they needed to separate from the Anglican Church. Imagine their consternation when John Lyford, an Anglican minister, was sent by the investors to Plymouth in 1624. After lying about his faith and joining the Plymouth church, Lyford held Anglican services. Then he wrote letters to England, attacking Bradford and Separatism. Fed up with Lyford's actions, the colony's men voted to banish the minister.

A Pilgrim church service. Almost all illustrations of the Pilgrims depict men dressed in black suits and women in dark shapeless dresses. When not in church, however, men usually wore leather or woolen breeches, a long-sleeved shirt, a leather jacket, and—during cold weather—a cloak and a stocking cap. Women wore colorful ankle-length dresses, petticoats, and aprons. Children dressed like the adults, except for small boys, who wore a dress-like garment, called a coat, until about age six.

new settlers landed north of Plymouth on the shores of the Massachusetts Bay Colony.

While Bradford was happy that Plymouth had lighted the way for the Puritans, their arrival caused a great upheaval in his colony. Farmers suddenly had a new market for their corn and cattle, so prices began to rise. To increase their profits, farmers now wanted more land and they gradually began leaving Plymouth. Although Bradford welcomed the Puritans and maintained friendly relations with their leaders, in his heart he began to believe Plymouth was a failure.

Governor Bradford continued to oversee Plymouth's everyday operations as the town became dwarfed by the vast numbers of Puritans flocking to the Massachusetts Bay Colony. In addition to managing Plymouth's affairs, Bradford was the colony's treasurer and the main judge. He also made allotments of land and oversaw farming and defense. A diplomat to other colonies and Indian tribes, Bradford made treaties with nearby Indians. When it became necessary, he sent soldiers to fight in the devastating Pequot War (1636-1637), in which thousands of English settlers were killed and the Pequot Indians were wiped out.

Even as Bradford governed the colony, he also became its historian. He started writing *Of Plymouth Plantation* in 1630 and continued his chronicle until 1651. After completing that task, he found time to study Hebrew and compose poetry.

William Bradford stayed in office almost until his death, on May 9, 1657, at age 67. Although he had received no pay beyond trading privileges during most of his long service to the colony, he died a relatively rich man. His estate included a home in Plymouth, a second house a few miles away in what would become Kingston, and several parcels of land. Among his other possessions were three beer mugs, linen, pewter dishes, furniture, an extensive library, and such fine articles of clothing as a red cloak and waistcoat, a violet cloak, and two hats.

Late in his life, Governor William Bradford described the ties that bound the Pilgrims at Plymouth together as a "sacred bond." The success of Plymouth in Bradford's lifetime owed much to his commitment to this bond.

"And no man now thought he could live except he had cattle and a great deal of ground to keep them. . . . By which means they were scattered all over the Bay quickly and the town in which they lived compactly till now was left very thin and in a short time almost desolate."
—William Bradford

The first page of Bradford's manuscript, Of Plymouth Plantation

28

Chapter Two

John Winthrop
and the
Massachusetts Bay Colony

On a spring day in 1630, a 42-year-old English Puritan stood before a group on the deck of a large, three-masted ship. The ship was the *Arbella*, the flagship of a fleet carrying Puritan settlers from England to North America. As the *Arbella* heaved its way through the Atlantic Ocean, the Englishman delivered a sermon about what he hoped the Puritans would accomplish in their new home.

"We shall be as a city upon a hill," he pronounced. "The eyes of all people are upon us." As if he were aware of their future place in history, he continued, "If we shall deal falsely with our God in this work we have undertaken, and so cause him to withdraw his present help from us, we shall be made a story and a byword through the world."

By the end of the summer of 1630, a total of 16 ships—including the *Arbella*—had left England for the Massachusetts Bay Colony. These ships carried more than 1,000 Puritans—about three times as many colonists as had moved to Plymouth in the previous decade.

John Winthrop (1588-1649) devoted his fortune and the better part of his life to the Massachusetts Bay Colony.

Queen Elizabeth I of England (1533-1603) was also known as the "Virgin Queen" because she never married, despite having many suitors. Even at a time when women had almost no legal rights, Queen Elizabeth was an extraordinarily popular ruler.

Marriages among the middle and upper classes in England in Winthrop's time were arranged by parents. When a boy and girl married, the parents of each gave the couple land, money, and goods. The feelings of the couple might be considered, but marriages were more like business transactions than love matches.

The Puritans had a weighty mission. John Winthrop, the man who spoke that day, would toil for the rest of his life to build his "city upon the hill" in the land that would become the state of Massachusetts.

The only son of Adam and Anne Winthrop, John Winthrop was born on January 12, 1588. At that time, England was ruled by Queen Elizabeth I. The nation's exploration and trade were creating prosperity for the English ruling class, including the Winthrops, who had extensive estates in Suffolk.

We know little about John's early years, but he surely lived a privileged life as the son of a wealthy man. At age 15, John enrolled in Cambridge University's Trinity College, where he remained a student for two years. Later, he spent about a year studying law at Gray's Inn, then England's leading law school.

In April 1605, at the age of 17, John married 21-year-old Mary Forth, the only child of wealthy landowners. In the next decade, the couple had four children who survived infancy: John Jr., Henry, Forth, and Mary. Then, in 1615, John's wife died in childbirth, along with her newborn.

It was at about this time that Winthrop became a Puritan. Even as a boy he had been religiously inclined, and now he embraced Puritan beliefs wholeheartedly. He also began what would become a lifelong practice of keeping a detailed diary of his activities and his religious feelings and thoughts.

Not long after Mary's death, Winthrop wed Thomasine Clopton. But about a year later, in late

November of 1616, Thomasine died from complications of childbirth. Their baby daughter also died shortly after birth.

Winthrop married for a third time in the spring of 1618. Margaret Tyndal, a devout Puritan like himself, would bear four sons. Their relationship lasted nearly 30 years and was full of mutual respect, love, and understanding.

In the first decade of his marriage to Margaret, Winthrop devoted most of his energy to managing the property his father had turned over to him before their wedding. He served for years as a county justice of the peace, and he also spent time in London, where, in 1627, he obtained a position as a lawyer in one of the government's courts.

Puritans in England were subject to increasing persecution in the 1620s. Under the rule of King Charles I, Puritan preachers were jailed, and many Puritans who had enjoyed a high social standing suddenly found themselves in disfavor. In 1629, Winthrop lost his government position. Suddenly, his future was uncertain, and he could see that Puritans like him would never find freedom under the rule of King Charles. Winthrop was convinced that England was on a sinful path.

Other Puritans agreed. A group of Puritans had taken over a trading company known as the New England Company in early 1628. In June, under the leadership of a former soldier named John Endecott, this group sent about 40 settlers to found a colony at Salem, Massachusetts. Winthrop became involved two months later, even before losing his

In the 1600s, many women died in childbirth and many infants did not survive. A man who was widowed and left with small children to raise often remarried quickly, usually to a woman much younger than himself.

"I am . . . persuaded, God will bring some heavy affliction upon this land, and that speedily; but be of good comfort. . . . If the Lord sees it will be good for us, He will provide a shelter and a hiding place for us and others."
—John Winthrop to his wife, Margaret, 1629

The religious zeal of John Endecott (c.1588-1665) was both his strength and his weakness. He became governor two years before Winthrop came to Massachusetts. Endecott would later perpetrate brutal attacks on Indians and Quakers in the Massachusetts Bay Colony.

job. The New England Company had grander plans by this point. It set out to establish a large Puritan colony in the New World.

On March 4, 1629, the company, now renamed the Massachusetts Bay Company, received a royal charter to a colony in New England. This charter gave the Puritans the right to settle and govern the Massachusetts Bay Colony. Although the grant was not entirely specific about who received voting rights, the shareholders could choose a governor, a deputy governor, and a board of directors, known as "assistants," in annual elections. Four times a year the shareholders of the company would meet to make laws at their General Court.

The Puritan Way

John Winthrop knew the Puritan path was not an easy one to follow. In his journal, he wrote what he called a "conversation" with God. "Thou tell me," he confided in God, "and all experience tells me, that in this way there is the least company, and that those which do walk openly in this way shall be despised, pointed at, hated of this world." But, he added, he knew he was "in a right course . . . the narrow way that leads to heaven."

Many people think Puritans were people who found all pleasure sinful. This was not the case at all. Puritans enjoyed good food, alcoholic beverages (in moderation), the joy of love, and the pleasures of sex in marriage. Puritans, however, did believe that service to God was more important than anything else in life. To the Puritan way of thinking, even while enjoying the pleasures of the world, a person's mind should always be focused on God.

Central to Puritan beliefs was the idea that no matter how hard a person tried, gaining salvation was impossible unless one had been selected by God before birth—a religious concept known as predestination. Despite this, Puritans tried to perform good works and obey moral laws to demonstrate their salvation. Often this practice led to an assumption that people who were upright and successful were saved.

In the New World, Puritans quickly became as intolerant as King Charles. So-called "heretics" who disagreed with leaders of the church or the colony were punished or banished. Some of these troublemakers—including Roger Williams, Anne Hutchinson, and John Wheelwright—went on to found colonies of their own.

Just as the Pilgrims rarely called themselves Pilgrims, the Puritans did not call themselves Puritans. Instead, they called themselves the "people of God."

Typically, when a royal charter was issued to a trading company, a city in England was designated as the company's headquarters. Company officials in that city would be in charge of the far-off colony and would send a governor to serve as its leader. Somehow—perhaps simply by mistake—the charter issued to the Massachusetts Bay Company contained no such provision. Winthrop and the other Puritans decided to carry their charter with them instead. They hoped this would put the colony beyond the king's control.

Seven months after the Massachusetts Bay Company received its charter, Winthrop was elected the company's governor. He immediately began making preparations for the Puritans' departure for America. During the next few months, he arranged for ships and supplies and recruited Puritan men and women for the colony. He also enlisted as settlers many non-Puritan craftspeople who could build houses and ships and provide other needed skills.

On April 8, 1630, the *Arbella* set sail. It was the flagship of a fleet of 11 ships. Winthrop was accompanied by two of his sons, Henry and Stephen. Margaret, who was pregnant, remained behind with the other children. The ships in the first wave of vessels sailing to the Massachusetts Bay Colony (or Bay Colony) carried some 700 Puritans along with about 240 cattle, 60 horses, and supplies and materials to clear and plant land and build homes.

Two months after their departure from England, the Puritans knew they were nearing land. "We now had fair sunshine weather," Winthrop wrote in his journal, "and there came a smell off the shore like the smell of a garden."

At first, the new arrivals settled in at Charlestown, a few miles from Salem. A lack of fresh spring water in that location forced a quick move to the nearby site of present-day Boston.

"O, how loath am I to bid thee farewell, but since it must be, farewell, my sweet love, farewell. Farewell my dear children and family, the Lord bless you all, and grant me to see your faces once again."
—John Winthrop to Margaret, April 1630

Henry Winthrop's drowning a few days after landing was an omen of things to come. The Puritans were not prepared for the harsh conditions they had to endure in their new home. Most lived in rough tents that provided little shelter from rain, let alone the cold, snowy weather of the winter that followed. Although Winthrop sent out parties to trade for corn with local Native Americans, food was scarce. Many settlers were laid low by scurvy, a disease caused by their poor diet.

The settlers' first winter in America was terrible. Realizing there would be a shortage of food before crops could be harvested, Winthrop had sent a ship, the *Lyon*, back to England for supplies. But the ship had not yet returned, and only a few of the wealthier colonists—including Winthrop—had brought enough food to last until harvest time. Others had embarked with little more than their faith. Those who still had food shared their rations with the hungry.

The *Lyon* finally returned in February 1631, after Winthrop had given away his last handful of flour. By then, however, about 200 of the colonists had died from starvation, illness, and the cold. Eighty settlers who had suffered enough went back to England with the ship.

With the coming of spring, life in the colony improved. Fields were cleared, crops planted, and permanent houses began replacing tents and wigwams. A church was formed with John Wilson as preacher. In late 1631, Margaret arrived with the rest of the Winthrops' children.

At first, many settlers in the colony lived in tents and wigwams like those made by local American Indians. These wigwams were made of bent poles covered by branches. Some dug burrows with branches laid over the top or lived in caves. One man even took shelter in an empty barrel.

Aboard the *Lyon* when it arrived in the Bay Colony in 1631 was Roger Williams, described by Winthrop as a "godly minister." Williams was to go on to stir up controversy in the colony and would ultimately become the founder of Rhode Island.

The Puritans and the Indians

Like the Pilgrims, the Puritans at first peacefully coexisted with the Native Americans in the region, partly because the few natives in the region were soon outnumbered by the English settlers. But the Puritans, by and large, did treat the Native Americans with respect. More than one settler was apprehended and punished for mistreating the original inhabitants of the territory. A settler named Nicholas Frost, for example, was fined, whipped, branded on the hand, and banished for stealing from the local Indians as well as for other crimes. And Massachusetts Bay Colony officials ordered Charlestown to pay damages after some pigs belonging to townspeople ate an Indian's corn.

The tribes of the Bay Colony were also fairly treated by the Puritans when it came to dealings over land. Most of the time, the Puritans, like the Pilgrims, paid a fair price for land they wanted. In many cases, they even gave the tribes that sold the land the right to continue hunting and fishing there. Still, as the number of settlers grew rapidly during the 1630s, friction increased between the settlers and the natives. In 1636 and 1637, the Bay Colony and other colonies in the region became embroiled in what is now known as the Pequot War.

The massacre of the Pequots in that war served as a terrible warning to other tribes not to interfere with English colonization. For the next 40 years, Indians mostly let the English settle where they pleased.

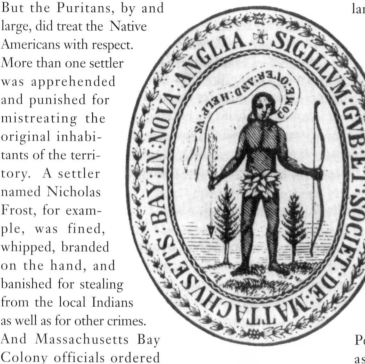

The official seal of the Massachusetts Bay Colony showed an Indian calling, "Come over and help us"— wishful thinking on the part of Puritans, who were not very successful as missionaries.

Under Winthrop's guidance, one of the first acts of the colony's leaders was to give colonists a voice in their own government. The few shareholders in Massachusetts had transferred their powers to the assistants. Now 118 adult male church members were also made assistants and given the right to vote for the elective offices and make laws at the General Court. Even though Winthrop was a typical Englishman of his class, he knew that the colonists would follow authority more readily if they had at least some influence in the selection of their leaders.

From the colony's earliest days, Winthrop was popular with most of the settlers. He was reelected to the position of governor in 1631, 1632, and 1633. During those years, as thousands of Puritans came to North America, new settlements were founded in Massachusetts at Lynn, Medford, Watertown, Dorchester, and Roxbury. Thanks to Winthrop's foresight in bringing shipbuilders to the new land, overseas trade quickly began to flourish.

While the Massachusetts Bay Colony thrived under Winthrop, it was not without conflict. Many disagreements were about religion; others had to do with the way the colony was governed. Usually, Winthrop was able to resolve disputes through reason even though he had the power, under the colony's charter, to demand compliance.

In 1631, for example, George Phillips, the minister of the Puritan church in Watertown, preached that the Roman Catholic Church was also a true Christian church. This was a dangerous opinion for the Puritans because it threw into question

Despite the close ties between church and government leaders in the Massachusetts Bay Colony, the Puritans were vigilant about some forms of separation of church and state. Ministers were forbidden to run for government office, and the government could not interfere with church decisions. Only church members, however, had voting rights.

Winthrop wrote in his journal that in the early days of a colony "justice should be administered with more leniency than in a settled state, because people were then more apt to transgress, partly of ignorance of new laws and orders."

The Puritans were serious about law enforcement. People faced whipping or the stocks, as shown here, for misdeeds as minor as lying or failing to attend church services. After confinement in the stocks, offenders were often required to wear a sign announcing their crime in front of the church.

their whole effort to purify the Anglican Church of Catholic elements. As governor, Winthrop could have ordered Phillips brought to trial and banished. Instead, he went to Watertown and debated with the minister until he convinced him of the error of his thinking.

The following year, Phillips was at the center of another conflict when he and Richard Brown, one of the members of his church, refused to pay taxes levied by the assistants to build defenses in another town. They believed the government should not tax without the people's consent. In response, Winthrop reminded the men that they had the right

to vote for any man as assistant. If they did not approve of an assistant's action, they could vote to remove him from office. Once again, reason prevailed and Winthrop did not punish the men.

Even though Phillips and Brown backed down, Winthrop apparently thought their concerns about taxation had merit. Soon after his conflict with the two men, Winthrop approved a change in government. Two representatives, known as deputies, would be chosen from each district to confer with the governor before any taxes were levied. Now the government of the colony consisted of a governor, a deputy governor, a group of assistants, and a group of deputies. Over time, this form of government would evolve to an upper and lower house of representatives, which became the structure in place today at the national level and in most states.

At the same meeting, Winthrop urged that the voters be allowed to elect the governor and deputy governor. After much argument with the current assistants, who did not want to give up their power to choose the colony's most important leaders, the proposal became law.

While Winthrop was popular with most colonists, he came under fire from the influential deputy governor, Thomas Dudley, for being too lenient in dealing with wrongdoers like Phillips and Brown. Dudley and many other Puritan leaders believed government should enforce good behavior and obedience to all laws, including requiring church attendance. Caving in to the pressure, Winthrop promised to be more strict in the future. This change in policy would have a tremendous impact on the development of the northeastern colonies.

Despite Winthrop's popularity, many colonists worried that he might become governor for life. They had endured enough of that kind of authority in England and wanted to avoid it in Massachusetts. In 1634, he was voted out of office. He was, however, elected an assistant, a position he held for three years as Thomas Dudley, then John Haynes, and finally Henry Vane sat in the governor's chair.

While Winthrop had governed the colony with restraint, Thomas Dudley and John Haynes were more heavy-handed. Haynes, like Dudley, had rebuked Winthrop for being too easygoing in his dealings with the colonists. The next few years would test the efforts of all the leaders as a new conflict almost tore Massachusetts apart.

Not surprisingly, this conflict was about religion. At the center of the dispute were the so-called "Antinomians," who believed they received direct revelations from God and were saved by God's grace. Observing civil or moral laws, they argued, was thus no evidence of salvation because only God granted salvation. Winthrop and other Puritan leaders were appalled by this challenge to their authority. They saw civic leaders as doing God's work and insisted that observance of the law was required of all godly men and women. Allowing Antinomians the freedom to practice their beliefs in Massachusetts might destroy the colony.

The leader of the Antinomians in the Bay Colony was Anne Hutchinson. Strong-willed and

Antinomian, a term from the Greek words "anti-" and "nomos" (or law), means opposed to moral law.

highly intelligent, Hutchinson was a gifted speaker who was not afraid to make her beliefs known. Soon she attracted a large following—including Governor Henry Vane.

Winthrop was alarmed at the growing power of Hutchinson and the Antinomians. After being elected governor again in the spring of 1637, he wrote carefully reasoned arguments in the hope of convincing the Antinomians of their error and bringing them back to the true path of Puritanism. But nothing worked. Finally, as the conflict divided the colony into two camps, there was no course of action but to bring Hutchinson and her followers to trial.

The story of Winthrop's role in that trial is not pleasant. He was a harsh judge. Undoubtedly, he remembered how he had been criticized for leniency during his previous terms as governor. At the same time, he fervently believed Antinomianism would destroy the Massachusetts Bay Colony. In spite of the fact that Anne Hutchinson brilliantly responded to all of his arguments, power was on the side of Winthrop. He simply dismissed her answers at the two-day trial and denied her the right to interpret sermons and the Bible. Ultimately, Hutchinson and several of her followers were banished from the Bay Colony.

While Winthrop's role in this controversy is troubling from a modern point of view, his defeat of Hutchinson was a victory for Puritanism. Just a year later, the governor was able to say "all breaches were made up, and the church was saved from ruin beyond all expectation."

John Winthrop remained at the center of both government and religion in Massachusetts for the rest of his life. Every year until his death, he was elected either governor, deputy governor, or assistant. Winthrop's views, however, often clashed with the people's desire for a more democratic government. Despite his opposition, the Body of Liberties became in 1641 the first set of laws governing the Bay Colony. And, in 1644, a representative government with a two-house legislature was instituted.

Winthrop was not always on the losing side of government decisions. In 1643, he saw an idea he had first proposed almost a decade earlier become reality when the Puritan colonies of Massachusetts, New Haven, and Connecticut joined with Plymouth

In 1646, this battery mounting 13 cannons was built on the wharf in Boston to defend the Massachusetts Bay Colony.

in a confederation to provide protection against attack by Indians or by the Dutch and French who had colonies nearby. Non-Puritan colonies such as Rhode Island were not invited to join. While Plymouth went further in its defiance of the Church of England than the Massachusetts Bay Colony was willing to go, it was included in what was known as the Confederation of New England.

The Bay Colony flourished in Winthrop's years, and Boston became the largest city and the center of trade in New England. The first influx of settlers fueled the colony's growth until 1640. Then, when the English Civil War in the 1640s slowed the surge of new colonists, the government was able to open up overseas trade so the colonists could still produce goods profitably.

Margaret was by Winthrop's side during all these years. But an epidemic, probably influenza, swept through New England in 1647, killing hundreds of people. Among the victims was Margaret, the woman Winthrop called "the faithful companion of my pilgrimage."

Within a year, Winthrop had married again. His fourth wife, Martha, was the daughter of a naval officer and was herself a widow. She bore him one son, who died in early childhood.

In the spring of 1649, less than two years after Margaret's death, John Winthrop died at the age of 61. At the center of Massachusetts Bay Colony events for his 19 years in the New World, his life was inseparable from the colony's history.

King Charles I (1600-1649), who had driven the Puritans from England, died the same year as John Winthrop. He was beheaded by the Puritans who took over the English government in 1649.

Massachusetts: From Settlements to Statehood

Because Puritans had gained power in England, few new colonists came to Massachusetts in the years following the death of John Winthrop in 1649. The lack of new markets for their cattle ruined Plymouth farmers, but the Massachusetts Bay Colony still remained stable. Settlers established a strong economy based on farming, logging, fishing and shipbuilding.

In 1660, however, the Bay Colony, which included not only Boston and Salem, but also much of New Hampshire and Maine, entered a period of turmoil. The Puritan government in England was overthrown that year and the English monarchy was restored. For the next three decades, during the monarchies of King Charles II and then James II, there were continual disagreements between the settlers and England. Finally, in 1684, King James II revoked the colony's charter. Two years later, he named Sir Edmund Andros, New York's former governor, to be the colonial governor of what was called the Dominion of New England. Andros was hated by the Bay Colony citizens.

James II was every bit as unpopular in England as Andros was in the Bay Colony. In 1688, the king was deposed from the throne in what was known as the Glorious Revolution. Soon after word reached America that the king had lost power,

Sir Edmund Andros (1637-1714)

colonists removed Andros from office and imprisoned him. He was sent back to England in 1690.

The next year, the Puritans finally got a royal charter protecting the colony again. Plymouth Colony, the oldest settlement in the Northeast, was legally absorbed by the Massachusetts Bay Colony in this charter. While Bay Colony leaders were pleased to have the newly expanded colony secured, they did not like having to serve under a governor appointed by the monarch.

Although the Bay Colony continued to thrive economically, Puritanism was on the wane by the dawn of the eighteenth century. Each generation of Puritans was less devout than the one before, and the tragic Salem Witch Trials of 1692 made the religion seem dangerously superstitious. In time, Puritan and Separatist churches were transformed into the modern Baptist, Congregationalist, and Unitarian churches that remain active across the United States to this day.

The growing wealth of Massachusetts (and other English colonies) in the 1700s attracted the attention of the British government, which was hungry for revenue. In the 1760s, the British treasury began heavily taxing the colonists. These taxes were especially unpopular in Massachusetts. The colonists' resentment of being taxed by officials who didn't represent them ultimately led to the Revolutionary War.

Massachusetts was at the center of the action when the Revolutionary War started in 1775. The famous battles of Lexington and Concord were fought on its soil, and Massachusetts leaders were central in the planning of a new, independent nation. In February 1788, Massachusetts became the sixth state to join the United States.

At the Boston Tea Party in 1773, colonists destroyed tea to protest paying taxes on the product.

46

Chapter Three

Peter Stuyvesant
and
Dutch New York

O n a May day in 1647, a tall, peg-legged man made his way down a boat's gangplank and stepped ashore in the village of New Amsterdam, the capital city of the colony the Dutch called New Netherland. The man was dressed in a jacket with silver buttons, and a broadsword hung at his waist. The wooden leg he wore in place of his right leg, which had been shot off in battle, was decorated with silver bands and nails. He was, one observer said, "like a peacock, with great state and pomp."

Thirty-seven-year-old Peter Stuyvesant had come to America to serve as New Netherland's director-general. For the next 17 years he ruled the colony with an iron hand and a fiery temper. Some of those who lived under his rule would call him "Old Silvernails" in honor of his flashy wooden leg.

Although Peter Stuyvesant (1610-1672) was unpopular with the colonists, he built a city that is now one of the world's greatest.

New York: Discovery and Early Settlement

The first European to view what is today the state of New York was probably John Cabot, a Portuguese captain sailing under the English flag. In 1497, he sailed south from Labrador along the east coast of North America and almost certainly ventured into the mouth of what is now the Hudson River.

Cabot, however, did not explore the river. That adventure was left to Henry

Henry Hudson (in the dark suit at left) talks with Indians on the Hudson River.

Hudson, an Englishman sailing for the Dutch East India Company. In 1609, Hudson made his way up the great river that now bears his name. He was searching for what hopeful explorers called the Northwest Passage—a shorter, more direct route to the East Asian countries that were rich in trading goods such as spices and tea desired by the Europeans. Instead, he discovered lush, fertile lands and American Indians, probably Mohicans, who were willing to trade. Upon his return to Europe, he gave the Dutch a glowing report of the land. Within two years, fur-trading ships were sailing regularly between Amsterdam and what was then New Netherland.

In about 1613, determined to protect their claim from the English, the Dutch set out to build permanent colonies along both the Hudson River and the Delaware River to the south. They built a few cabins on Manhattan Island and established a fort and trading post near what is now Albany, the capital of the state of New York. In 1623, a ship sent by the newly organized Dutch West India Company arrived with 30 families. The Dutch then built Fort Orange on the ruins of the neglected fort near Albany so the colonists would have protection. The settlement of New Netherland was firmly established—at least for a time.

The first Dutch settlement on Manhattan Island

Others called him "Stubborn Pete" because of his temperament. Not a few people called him a tyrant, or worse. Yet, in his nearly two decades in power, Stuyvesant turned the village of New Amsterdam into a flourishing trading center that would ultimately become New York City. In the process, he earned his place as one of America's great colonists.

Peter was born to Balthazar and Margaretta Stuyvesant in 1610 in the northwest region of the Netherlands known as Friesland. Although little is known of Peter's youth, we do know his father was a minister in a small town, so we can assume that Peter and his older sister, Anna, did not enjoy a life of luxury. We also know their mother died when Peter was about 15.

At the age of 20, Peter enrolled in a small university in the town of Franeker, not far from his home. Just two years later, however, he was expelled from the school, reportedly for seducing his landlord's daughter.

After leaving Franeker, Stuyvesant went to the capital city of Amsterdam, where he found employment as a clerk with the Dutch West India Company. He spent several years supervising the company's shipping cargo in Brazil. By 1643, he was the director of operations on the Caribbean island of Curaçao. The next year, he was ordered by the company to attack the Caribbean island of Saint Martin and take it from the Spanish. In March 1644, he set sail with 300 soldiers. Stuyvesant's army was soundly beaten in the battle for the tiny island, and his right leg was so badly wounded it had to be amputated.

By 1610, the English colony of Jamestown in Virginia was already three years old.

The Dutch West India Company was established in 1621 by the government of the Netherlands to manage Dutch land in the Americas, Australia, and West Africa. The company was given the sole right to claim new territories, make treaties, build forts, and govern settlers. It made most of its fortune attacking and looting Spanish ships.

Stuyvesant returned to the Netherlands to recuperate from his operation. There, he met Judith Bayard. Judith's brother was married to Stuyvesant's sister, Anna. A romance blossomed. On August 13, 1645, Stuyvesant walked down the wedding aisle sporting his fancy new wooden leg.

In Amsterdam, Stuyvesant heard that the Dutch West India Company was looking for someone to govern the struggling and widely scattered New Netherland. He offered his services. A year after his marriage, he was appointed director-general of the colony, including its Caribbean territories.

On Christmas Day, 1646, Peter and Judith Stuyvesant set sail for the New World on the flagship of a small fleet. After a stopover in Curaçao, the four ships of the fleet arrived in the New Netherland harbor on May 11, 1647. Stuyvesant was met by a crowd waiting to catch a glimpse of the new director-general. Cheers filled the air as he entered the city with Willem Kieft, the man he was replacing. The crowd had reason to cheer, for Kieft, who had ruled for eight years, had nearly destroyed the colony when he started a bloody war with the Delaware Indians and other local tribes.

In a speech that day, Stuyvesant declared that he wished to act "as a father" to the colonists. The Dutch military hero would face his greatest challenge in convincing these people of widely varying backgrounds—they spoke 18 different languages—to work together to create a stable colony. It also would soon be obvious that Stuyvesant's first loyalty was to the company, not to the colony or the colonists.

New Netherland's Rulers

By 1624, the Dutch West India Company was determined to establish a permanent trading center in what we know as New York. Cornelis May established Fort Orange at Albany that year, but he was replaced the next year by Willem Verhulst. Two years later, Verhulst was succeeded by Peter Minuit, who served as director-general from 1626 until 1632. Minuit realized that the real center of the colony was Manhattan Island instead of Fort Orange. Soon after his arrival in New Netherland, he purchased the island from a local group of Native Americans for about $24 worth of trade goods. The land bought by Minuit for beads and other trinkets is today some of the most valuable real estate in the world. Minuit later used the knowledge he gained as director-general of New Netherland to found New Sweden on the banks of the Delaware River.

Minuit was replaced in 1633 by Wouter van Twiller, who served for about five years until he was relieved by Willem Kieft. Of all the leaders who preceded Stuyvesant, Kieft was the worst. He almost single-handedly started a war between the Dutch settlers and the Indian tribes living south of the Hudson River. In this war, scores of colonists were killed and their homes and farms burned, while almost a thousand Indians, including women and children, were massacred. Having nearly destroyed his colony, Kieft was finally removed from office in 1646, to be replaced the following year by Stuyvesant.

Indeed, the cheering soon stopped for the new director-general. Within a few weeks of his arrival, Stuyvesant was embroiled in a dispute with two important landowners. These men, Jochem Kuyter and Cornelis Melyn, made the mistake of complaining to Stuyvesant about former director-general Kieft. If such men could challenge one ruler, Stuyvesant reasoned, they could challenge him as well. To get rid of potential troublemakers, he ordered the two men banished from the colony for supposedly seditious behavior. This act turned the colony against him.

But Stuyvesant believed New Netherland was in need of a firm leader. The Dutch had once claimed a large territory that stretched from the Saint Lawrence River in the north to Cape Cod in the northeast and the Delaware River on the south. Thanks to mismanagement by the governors before Stuyvesant, New Netherland had shrunk to just a few scattered pieces of land, including Manhattan Island, part of Long Island, an outpost on the Delaware River, and an already decaying Fort Orange. Most of the 1,500 colonists in the New Netherland region lived in a collection of rough wooden buildings on New Amsterdam's narrow dirt streets. Fort Amsterdam, the town's main protection, was falling down, and goats and sheep grazed on top of its crumbling earthen walls. The church in the fort—the colony's only religious establishment—was in ruins. Nearly every fourth shop in the town was a tavern and public drunkenness was common.

Almost as soon as he arrived in America, Stuyvesant set about reforming the settlement to make it a real community. This was difficult since most colonists did not consider the colony a permanent home. In addition, New Netherland lacked professional farmers and had a scarcity of skilled craftspeople. But Stuyvesant had to try.

Some of his laws were meant to improve public morals. He outlawed the sale of liquor to Indians, and he restricted the hours that taverns could operate. He also put in place a tax on liquor and wine to

Stuyvesant punished Kuyter and Melyn to show the people of the colony, especially those in New Amsterdam, he was boss. "These churls may hereafter endeavor to knock me down also," he warned, "but I will manage it so . . . they will have their bellies full [of trouble]" if they do.

Manhattan Island got its name from an Indian word for "island of the hills." When settlers first saw the island, they admired its lush meadows and its forests thick with wild game. Today it is one of the most densely populated places in the world.

53

pay for repairs to Fort Amsterdam and its church. A devout—and intolerant—member of the Dutch Reformed Church, Stuyvesant banned business on Sundays, required church attendance, and outlawed some other religions.

Other laws attempted to regulate business and trade for the company's benefit. Stuyvesant infuriated colonists by imposing a 30 percent tax on imports and exports. Then he took steps to keep settlers from illegally trading with Native Americans and smuggling furs outside the colony—activities that evaded taxation.

New Amsterdam was soon humming with activity under Stuyvesant's rule. Repairs were started on many of the city's buildings, and fences were built to keep livestock from wandering. The noise of hammers and saws, though, did not hide the sounds of grumbling among the colonists. Forced to curtail their drinking and carousing, unable to sell liquor or to trade furs, and taxed to pay for civic improvements, the colonists were angry.

To make his plans more acceptable, Stuyvesant told the people they could nominate 18 men to serve as his advisers. From that list of 18, he chose 9 who became the "Board of Nine Men" in September 1647. For the first time, the New Amsterdam colonists had a voice in their own government. It was not long, however, before Stuyvesant and the board were fighting. Much of the trouble seems to have been Stubborn Pete's fault. Under pressure for profits from the West India company, he treated the 9 men as if they were "rascals, liars, rebels,

"Mr. Stuyvesant has almost all the time from his first arrival . . . been busy building, laying masonry, making, breaking, repairing and the like."
—Adriaen van der Donck, *Representation of New Netherland*, 1650

usurpers and spendthrifts . . . [as if] hanging was almost too good for them," complained one board member.

That man was Adriaen van der Donck. Tired of the Dutch West India Company's tyranny, van der Donck, a lawyer, began to keep a record of the company's and the director-general's actions. By 1650, van der Donck had written a lengthy document called the *Representation of New Netherland*. This treatise spelled out the board's complaints against Stuyvesant and asked that the people of New Amsterdam be allowed to establish their own democratic government. Van der Donck sailed to Holland to present the report to the States-General, as the government of the Netherlands was then called.

It took the States-General more than two years to reach a decision, but, in 1652, New Amsterdam was granted a city government. The Board of Nine Men got no other satisfaction, however. At first, the States-General decided to recall Stuyvesant, but then they canceled the order. The director-general continued his rule without interruption.

While he was under attack in the Netherlands, Stuyvesant took steps to protect the colony from enemies closer at hand: the English and the Swedes. The more serious threat was posed by the English, who argued that the territory should be theirs because it was first explored in 1497 by John Cabot, who sailed under the English flag. This dispute about the Dutch claim emboldened English settlers in Connecticut to contest the boundary between New Netherland and their colony.

Adriaen van der Donck was known as "the Jonker" (pronounced "yonker"), or the young nobleman. His estate, about 15 miles north of New Amsterdam, was known as Jonker's Manor. Today that site is the city of Yonkers, New York.

In his *Representation of New Netherland*, Adriaen van der Donck complained bitterly about the way Stuyvesant treated the colonists. "For whoever [Stuyvesant] has him opposed," he wrote, "has as much as the sun and moon against him."

Once, when a colonist threatened to appeal a sentence handed down by Stuyvesant, the director-general warned that he would cut off the colonist's head: "I will . . . send the pieces to Holland, and let him appeal that way!"

In 1643, four of the New England colonies—Massachusetts, New Haven, Plymouth, and Connecticut—had formed a union known as the Confederation of New England. This union had authority to declare war, deal with Indian affairs, and settle disagreements between colonies.

In 1653, in response to rumors that the English colonies were preparing to attack New Amsterdam, Stuyvesant ordered the construction of a wall on the southern tip of Manhattan Island, enclosing most of the city. The wall provided little defense against the English attack a decade later, but a path that ran along the wall soon became known as Wall Street. Today, this street in the heart of New York City's financial district is one of the most famous in the world.

In 1650, Stuyvesant negotiated an agreement with the Confederation of New England. To keep peace with the English, however, Stuyvesant had to put a large part of the colony in English hands, including the eastern portion of Long Island. In the wake of this agreement, the director-general's popularity waned even further since many of the colonists thought the deal he struck was humiliating. The agreement did not even keep the peace for long. In 1653 and 1654, the confederation nearly went to war against New Netherland over boundary issues.

As soon as he thought he had resolved the dispute with the English, Stuyvesant turned to the Swedes. With the help of former New Netherland leader Peter Minuit, the Swedes had started a colony on the Delaware River. In 1651, Stuyvesant had tried to stop Swedish settlers from trespassing on the southern border of New Netherland by erecting a fort downriver from them. A fort between the Swedes and the ocean would have cut the Swedish settlement off from supply and trading vessels coming from Europe. That strategy failed three years later when the Swedes threatened to attack the fort with a fleet of ships, forcing its surrender.

Stuyvesant decided to end the Swedish threat once and for all in 1655. With an army of about 700 men, he sailed up the river to the Swedish settlement. Hopelessly outnumbered, the Swedes gave up. In victory, Stuyvesant was gracious. Although he shipped the leaders of the Swedish colony back to Europe, he allowed the settlers to stay—provided they swore allegiance to New Netherland.

Peter Minuit

Peter Minuit was a man on the move. In his short career, he served both the Netherlands and Sweden in their attempts to found colonies in the New World.

Minuit's own nationality is a mystery. Born in 1580 in a town called Wesel in what is now Germany, Minuit was probably of French descent. But he was fluent in Dutch and lived near the Dutch border. Sometimes his name was spelled Minnewit, the way the Dutch would have pronounced it.

Minuit served on the Director's Council under Willem Verhulst in New Netherland in 1625 and held a minor post there the next year. He was apparently surprised to be appointed New Netherland's first director-general in 1626.

With his purchase of Manhattan Island, Director-General Minuit strived to make New Amsterdam the center of the scattered settlements of the colony. He also started trading and diplomatic relations with Governor William Bradford and the colonists at Plymouth.

Despite Minuit's successes, he was called back to the Netherlands for review in 1631. He would not return to New Netherland, although his position was not filled until 1633.

A few years later, Minuit was called into service for Sweden. A Swedish company was founded in 1637 to establish a colony on Delaware Bay, which borders present-day Delaware and New Jersey. At the end of March in 1638, Peter Minuit purchased land on the western bank of the Delaware River from the local Delaware Indians. There he built Fort Christina, named after the queen of Sweden, on the site of the future city of Wilmington, Delaware. The Dutch Fort Nassau was only a few miles upriver.

Willem Kieft, the new director-general of New Netherland, sent a letter to Minuit to protest his encroachment on what the Dutch saw as their territory. Minuit ignored the letter, but his colonial career soon came to an end anyway. After the completion of Fort Christina, Peter Minuit sailed to the Caribbean on a trading mission. He was lost at sea in a hurricane.

Stuyvesant also demonstrated his leadership abilities upon his return from the expedition to New Sweden. At that time, hundreds of American Indians who lived near Manhattan attacked and looted New Amsterdam and other nearby settlements, killing about 50 settlers and taking some 100 more captive. The trouble had started when a settler shot and killed a Native American woman who was picking peaches in his orchard. In Stuyvesant's absence, a company official ordered a disastrous retaliatory attack, which led to massacres and destruction. On his return, Stuyvesant calmed the situation and negotiated peace in order to save the captives and prevent war, which the outnumbered Dutch would surely have lost.

New Netherland appeared to thrive during these years, despite the fact that many colonists were unhappy. Stuyvesant made defense his first priority, and he was convinced that New Netherland would not be secure until the population had increased and skilled tradespeople had come to meet the colonists' needs. New villages were established, including one at Harlem, several miles north of the center of the city of New Amsterdam.

New Amsterdam itself finally began to look like a city. There were almost three times as many houses in 1660 as in 1656, and the population had increased by 50 percent in those same years. Stuyvesant worked hard to convince ministers to move there and schoolteachers to come to educate the settlers' children. Under his leadership, the Dutch Reformed church within the fort was

repaired, a wharf was built in one of the city's harbors, and a large, block-long market was constructed
where traders and settlers could sell their wares. To
manage the growth, the director-general instituted
fire-control measures and established public dump-
ing grounds. Still, because of its dependence on an
inefficient land-granting plan known as the "Patroon
System," New Netherland never flourished the way
the Massachusetts Bay Colony did.

  In 1657, the director-general was involved in a
dispute that may well have been the low point of his
rule. This conflict centered on Robert Hodgson, a
Quaker who had been expelled from Massachusetts

*The New Amsterdam that
Stuyvesant built. There were
1,500 people and 342 houses
in 1660, and the city was
becoming the center of trade
on the East Coast, with
English, French, and Spanish
vessels as well as Dutch ships
visiting its harbors.*

To entice people to leave prosperous Holland and develop farms in New Netherland, the West India Company offered huge tracts of land—the Northeast's only true plantations—to wealthy patrons in exchange for settling at least 50 persons on the land within four years. Under the Patroon System ("patroon" means "patron" in Dutch), settlers were indentured servants who received no pay for their work.

for practicing his religion. Hodgson came to Long Island, where he began preaching his religious beliefs to anyone who would listen.

Stuyvesant was an intolerant man in an intolerant era. He especially despised Quakers, perhaps because they refused to honor authority figures like himself or because they refused to bear arms even when the colony was threatened. Whatever the reason, as soon as he learned about Hodgson's actions, Stuyvesant had the Quaker arrested and flogged.

When other Quakers heard of Stuyvesant's treatment of Hodgson, they began holding their religious meetings openly, in defiance of the law. Stuyvesant ordered these men and women thrown in jail. Officials in the village of Flushing, where the Quakers were meeting, refused to follow his order.

Instead, they joined Flushing's Dutch and English citizens in signing a statement calling for religious tolerance. Not one to back down, Stuyvesant had these officials arrested. Some were jailed; others were dismissed from office, fined, or threatened with banishment from the colony. Finally, the Dutch West India Company stepped in. A letter to Stuyvesant reminded him that Holland itself was a religious haven. The company ordered him to leave the Quakers alone.

Stuyvesant had other nagging problems. During all the years of his rule, the colonists refused to pay to complete the repairs to Fort Amsterdam. Neither the West India Company nor the States-General wanted to spend money for defense of the colony. Despite repeated Indian attacks and threats

A Dutch farm in Leeds, New York, near the Hudson River north of New York City. The owner had this mural painted over his fireplace mantel.

The Dutch and the Indians

The first American Indians the Dutch met were probably the Mohicans, a tribe in the Algonquin confederacy, who were living on land around Fort Orange, near the site of present-day Albany. The Dutch also came in contact with the Mohawks, one of five tribes, or nations, in what was then known as the League of the Iroquois. The other tribes in the League were the Oneidas, the Onondagas, the Cayugas, and the Senecas. (A sixth tribe, the Tuscaroras, joined the league in the early eighteenth century.)

Fierce warriors, the Mohawks had driven other tribes from the fertile lands north of the Hudson by the time the Dutch arrived in America. Only the Algonquins were able to resist the Iroquois—because they were armed with muskets given to them by the French in Canada.

The Mohawks wanted to make the contest even. They made arrangements to trade beaver pelts to the Dutch for muskets and bullets. Always interested in profits, the Dutch were eager to trade with both the Mohawks and the Mohicans, prolonging the military conflict in the process. Prices were so good that some even traded their own guns, leaving themselves defenseless. The Dutch felt their best protection lay in making alliances with the Indians.

In 1618, shortly after the Fort Orange settlement was established, the Dutch signed a treaty with the Mohicans and probably with the Mohawks. The agreements provided the Dutch with protection on the frontier between New Netherland and French territories. After Kieft's disastrous war, Stuyvesant sought stable Indian relations, using the firearm trade and careful alliances to control problems that arose, including a 1660 war with the Esopus Indians, a branch of the Delaware Indians.

from other colonies, the authorities were interested in trading and profits and little else. The lack of military preparedness had serious consequences in 1664, when England decided to revive its claim to New Netherland. In that year, King Charles II of England simply gave the colony to his brother James, the duke of York (later King James II).

In late August 1664, four English ships under the command of Colonel Richard Nicolls anchored just outside New Amsterdam. On board the ships were hundreds of soldiers, ready to fight. The citizens of the city, perhaps because they had been treated so shabbily by the West India Company, quickly prepared to surrender. For a time, Stuyvesant tried to rally the people to fight. He tore up the surrender demand sent to him by Nicolls and ordered soldiers to repair the fort's walls. But his actions were too little, too late. On September 8, following a show of force by the English, Stuyvesant surrendered the colony, which was promptly renamed New York. Fifty-five years after Henry Hudson discovered Manhattan, the Dutch colonial presence in America came to an end.

When Peter Stuyvesant surrendered New Netherland, the entire East Coast from Maine to Florida came under the control of the English.

Colonel Richard Nicolls was generous to his new subjects. As New York's first governor, he gave the colony's residents 18 months to decide whether to remain, guaranteeing the rights of English citizenship to all colonists. Any Dutch custom that was not against English law would also be permitted. Most of the people stayed.

The spring following the surrender of New Netherland, Stuyvesant returned to Amsterdam. At first, he was blamed for all the misfortunes that had befallen the colony. Finally, however, he was cleared of charges of colonial mismanagement. Stuyvesant returned to New York and retired to his farm, or *bouwerie*, in an area now called the Bowery, about two miles north of modern-day Wall Street. There he spent the rest of his days as a farmer and a citizen of the town he had governed for 17 years. Peter Stuyvesant died in 1672 and was buried in a chapel on his farm.

New York: From Settlement to Statehood

Following the surrender of the colony to the British by Stuyvesant, the territory underwent rapid change. What is now New Jersey was separated from the rest of the colony. In 1665, the border between New York and Connecticut was established.

In 1688, New York and New Jersey were added to the New England colonies in the Dominion of New England under Sir Edmund Andros. Colonists in New York were no happier than their counterparts in Massachusetts under Andros's rule. When they heard the news of King James II's fall in the Glorious Revolution in England and the overthrow of Andros in Boston, they rebelled as well. For nearly two years, from 1689 to 1691, the colony was ruled by Jacob Leisler, a wealthy merchant who had led the rebellion. But in March 1691, the Crown reestablished control.

Since New York lay between French Canada to the north and the British colonies on the south, it was the site of many battles between the French and the British during the French and Indian War in the 1750s. Following the final defeat of the French in 1763, settlers from New England began to drift into New York, since they now felt safe there. As the population grew, manufacturing and trade expanded with it, adding economic strength to the former agricultural colony.

During the years of the American Revolution, New York was on center stage. About a third of the major battles of the war were fought in the colony. New York City was in British hands for most of the war, but the Americans won their first great battle at Saratoga, north of Albany, in October 1777, when British general John Burgoyne was forced to surrender.

Even while the Revolutionary War was still being fought in 1777, the state of New York was created by its citizens with a temporary capital at Kingston, north of New York City on the Hudson River. Albany became the state's capital in 1797. On July 26, 1788, New York was the eleventh of the 13 original states to ratify the new nation's constitution.

At Saratoga, New York, General John Burgoyne surrenders his sword to General Horatio Gates, commander of the American forces.

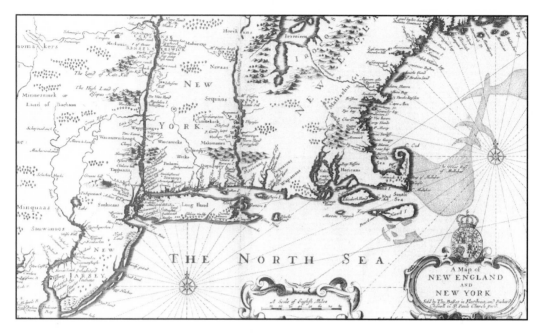

New York and New Jersey (spelled "New Iarsey") in 1676. Most of the regions were still designated by the names of the Indian tribes residing there.

New Jersey's Early Days

New Jersey shares much of its early history with the neighboring state of New York. Colonized by the Dutch West India Company and dotted with patroon landholdings, the territory was part of New Netherland. In 1655, Dutch holdings in New Jersey's Delaware Bay were increased when Peter Stuyvesant took New Sweden.

After Colonel Richard Nicolls conquered New Netherland for England in 1664 and made it New York, the colony of New Jersey became a complicated proprietorship—complicated because so many people held sometimes conflicting titles to parts of the territory.

James, the duke of York, granted New Jersey to George Carteret and John Berkeley, but Nicolls meanwhile had sold land to colonists from New England. Berkeley and Carteret split their holdings,

Sir George Carteret (c.1610-1680) was from the island of Jersey in England. He was also one of the proprietors of Carolina.

John Berkeley (1602-1678) won the king's gratitude for his heroism in the English Civil War with the Puritans in the 1640s. New Jersey was part of his belated reward.

with Berkeley taking West Jersey and Carteret East Jersey. Both proprietors were generous with land grants and allowed democratic forms of government, but the colonists who had purchased land from Nicolls still resisted the proprietors' claims to the land.

Intending to start a Quaker settlement in the years before Pennsylvania's founding, a group of English Quakers purchased West Jersey in 1674 and were rescued from financial disaster by William Penn and others in 1677. Penn and 11 other Quakers also bought Carteret's interest in East Jersey in 1681. But soon, the Quakers turned their attention to Pennsylvania.

Due to widespread resentment against the proprietors and confusions about their claims, the proprietors surrendered their power to govern New Jersey to the English monarch in 1702. Despite the fact that New Jersey was recognized as a separate colony from New York, it did not have its own governor until Lewis Morris assumed that position in 1738.

New Jersey declared itself a state in 1776 and was a major battleground during the American Revolution. It was the third state to ratify the U.S. Constitution.

Chapter Four

---◆◆◆---

Roger Williams
and the
Founding of Rhode Island

---◆◆◆---

On a bitterly cold January day in 1636, a Puritan preacher named Roger Williams trudged through the thick forest south of Salem in the Massachusetts Bay Colony. Just days before, Williams had been warned that he was about to be arrested for beliefs that endangered the colony's future. If he was caught, he knew he would be put on a ship and sent back to England. Williams fled into the wilderness and eventually made his way to Narragansett Bay. There, this radical minister attained lasting fame as founder of Rhode Island and the father of religious tolerance in North America.

Not much is known of Roger Williams's early life. We think he was born sometime in 1603. His father, James, was a tailor and merchant in London. His mother, Alice, was the daughter of a wealthy

At a time when Quakers were hanged in Massachusetts and Jews were widely persecuted in Europe, Roger Williams (c.1603-1683) welcomed both religious groups to Rhode Island.

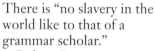

If Williams was born in 1603, he was lucky to have lived to celebrate his first birthday. That year, the plague stalked the streets of London. Of some 220,000 people living in the great city then, 30,000 died.

There is "no slavery in the world like to that of a grammar scholar."
—Robert Burton, an English writer who was in school at about the same time as Roger Williams

"This Roger Williams when he was a youth would in a shorthand take sermons, and speeches . . . and present them to my dear father, he seeing him so hopeful a youth, took such liking to him that he put him into [school]."
—Anne Sadleir, daughter of Sir Edward Coke

merchant. Her brother served for a time as the mayor of London. Roger had two brothers, one older and one younger, and an older sister.

Roger probably started school at about the age of six. As a student in London in the early 1600s, he would not have had much time for play. Students went to school six days a week, from about six in the morning until five in the evening, with just two short breaks for meals. Classes in reading, writing, Latin, logic, and the Bible were taught by stern teachers who believed school should be hard work instead of fun.

When Roger was about 14, he met Sir Edward Coke, a famous judge. According to legend, Roger was in church one Sunday taking shorthand notes of the pastor's sermon when he was seen by Coke. Impressed with the boy's skills, the judge hired him to take notes of judicial proceedings. For several years, Roger worked for Coke. With the judge's help, he was also able to continue his education. He attended Cambridge University, where he was first exposed to Puritanism. After receiving his undergraduate degree in January 1627, Williams remained at Cambridge for another two years, preparing to become a minister in the Anglican Church.

It was not unusual then for wealthy families with estates to have their own chapels and ministers, known as chaplains. In 1629, Williams was hired by Sir William Masham, a nobleman who lived in Essex in north-central England. By this time, Williams was, like Masham, a Puritan. At the estate, the young minister met such prominent Puritans as

Thomas Hooker and John Cotton. He also met Mary Barnard, a maid in the Masham household. On December 15, Roger and Mary were married. We don't know much about Mary. It is thought that she was about six years younger than Roger and was the daughter of a minister.

By the time Roger and Mary Williams wed, the Puritans throughout England were being persecuted by Anglican authorities. John Winthrop was already busy in the New World establishing the Massachusetts Bay Colony. Williams soon decided to join what would be known as the great Puritan Migration. On December 1, 1630, he and Mary set sail on board the *Lyon*, a ship bound for Winthrop's Massachusetts Bay Colony. Two months later, they arrived in Boston.

Almost from his first day in the Bay Colony, Williams was in conflict with the authorities. Offered a good job preaching in Boston, he turned the position down because the Boston church, unlike Plymouth's, had not separated from the Church of England. He further offended Bay Colony leaders by preaching that civil authorities had no business meddling in religious affairs. People, he said, should be allowed to worship as they pleased.

In spite of his "dangerous opinions," as the General Court invariably termed them, Williams briefly served as teacher at the church in Salem in 1631, but he left for the more hospitable Plymouth Colony later that year. In Plymouth, he befriended some local Indians. Desiring to convert them to Christianity, Williams also traded with them, learned

Sir Edward Coke (1552-1634) would suffer at the hands of the monarchy. At about the time he met Williams, he lost his position on the king's bench (which is like the U.S. Supreme Court) for supporting the rights of citizens against royal authority. Despite being fired, Coke remained a great advocate of citizens' rights.

their language, and started work on a dictionary of Indian words. Soon he began to question the justice of the royal charter granting Indian territory to Plymouth and the Massachusetts Bay Colony. This doubting offended Plymouth's authorities, and Williams returned to Salem in 1633.

For the next two years, the Puritan leaders tried to quiet the opinionated preacher. Despite their threats and arguments, Williams would not be muzzled. He preached what he believed to be the truth, even though it got him in trouble.

Williams's most dangerous opinion was that the king had no right to give away Indian lands in North America. Finally, in 1635, he committed what to the Puritans was an unpardonable act. He wrote a letter to King Charles I, telling the monarch he was evil for taking land from the Indians without payment. Although Williams was persuaded not to send the letter, Bay Colony authorities knew he was not to be trusted.

On October 9, 1635, at a hearing in Boston, the authorities fought back. This time, Williams had to answer for the content of two more letters. He had written one letter rebuking other Bay Colony churches for interfering with Salem church affairs. Then he attacked his own church in a second letter after Salem, under pressure from Bay Colony leaders, failed to back him. When Williams refused to retract his statements, the magistrates ordered him banished from the colony. They also warned him not to continue preaching his dangerous ideas during the six weeks before his deadline to leave.

Needless to say, Williams continued to preach. He also tried to convince some of his followers in Salem to join him in establishing a new colony south of Plymouth. As soon as the leaders of the Bay Colony heard of Williams's actions, they dispatched Captain John Underhill to take him into custody. This time, they would send the troublemaker back to England.

John Winthrop, who had always had a soft spot in his heart for Williams, secretly sent word to him that he was about to be arrested. In the dead of winter, the minister fled from Salem. Accompanied only by Thomas Angell, a young servant, Williams trudged south through the thick woods that surrounded the settlement. For days, he later said, he felt "sorely tossed" by fate as he and Angell made their way in the direction of the border between the Bay Colony and Plymouth Colony. In a letter he wrote when he was almost 70 years old, Williams called his journey into the wilderness a "sorrowful winter's flight" and said he had experienced cold he could "feel yet." Finally, they reached Sowam, the village of Chief Massasoit, the same Indian who had aided William Bradford and the Pilgrims.

Williams's friendship with the Wampanoag Indians who lived near Plymouth now saved his life. He and Angell were given food and shelter by Massasoit. For more than three months of a bitter winter, the pair stayed with the Indians.

When spring arrived, Williams moved on, settling on land he had purchased from Massasoit. This land was on the Seekonk River, near the site of what

"Whereas Mr. Roger Williams, one of the elders of the church of Salem, has broached and divulged diverse new and dangerous opinions against the authority of the magistrates, [and] also written letters of defamation both of the magistrates and churches here, it is therefore ordered, that the said Mr. Williams shall depart out of this jurisdiction within six weeks."
—from the order banishing Williams from Salem

When Williams fled into the woods, he left his wife and two daughters behind. The elder daughter, Mary, was about four. The younger girl, born at about the time Williams had his trial in Boston, was named Freeborn. Roger and Mary Williams later had two more children, Providence and Joseph.

is now Seekonk, Massachusetts. There he built a rough shelter of bent saplings covered by tree boughs. He then sent word to Salem, telling Mary of his whereabouts. Soon, Williams's wife and children joined him along with a small band of followers who had also been banished from the Bay Colony.

The newborn settlement near Seekonk was not to be successful, however. After they had planted their crops, Williams received word from Edward Winslow, then governor of Plymouth, that they were trespassing on his colony's territory. The rebel minister and his parishioners would have to move again.

Rhode Island's Beginnings

The first European to see Rhode Island may have been Miguel Corte Real, a Portuguese explorer who is believed to have sailed along the coast in 1511. About a dozen years later, Narragansett Bay was explored by Giovanni da Verrazano, an Italian explorer sailing under the flag of France. This bay, running north and south almost 30 miles from the Atlantic Ocean to the state capital of Providence, contains 36 islands that are part of what is now the state of Rhode Island. One of those islands is called Rhode Island, originally known as Aquidneck by the settlers and Indians. Block Island, also part of the state of Rhode Island, lies about 10 miles offshore. This island was named by the Dutch explorer Adriaen Block, who sailed along the coast early in the seventeenth century.

French and British sailors who fished off the coast of Massachusetts in the early 1600s almost certainly visited the coast of Rhode Island and probably came ashore to replenish their water supply and gather firewood. The area, however, was not settled by Europeans until 1636.

Rhode Island was Narragansett land. When Williams moved southwest of Massachusetts, out of Plymouth territory, he met with Narragansett chiefs to buy land.

Williams and several companions set out to find a new location for their settlement. They paddled a narrow canoe up the Seekonk River until Williams spied a likely spot. There, at the base of a hill near a freshwater spring, he decided to found his settlement.

Of course, they needed land. Believing as he did that the Indians should be paid for what was theirs, Williams purchased about 15 square miles of land from the Narragansett chiefs Canonicus and his nephew, Miantunomi. In exchange for the tract, he gave the Indians what he called "gratuities"— probably wampum (a form of money used by settlers and Indians), trinkets, and hand tools. He decided to call the settlement Providence.

At first, Williams and the other settlers in Providence lived in crude houses. More like bark-covered wigwams than cabins, these houses offered shelter, but little comfort. As soon as these buildings were finished, crops were planted. Even while the settlers waited for their crops to grow, they had plenty of food. The natives who lived nearby were willing to trade for grain, shellfish abounded in nearby Narragansett Bay, and game roamed the forests. Still, Providence was so poor that, on at least one occasion, John Winthrop quietly sent the settlers supplies and food.

From the start, Providence was very different from the colonies that preceded it. Plymouth and the Bay Colony had been founded by large groups, with financial backing from England and royal approval. Providence, in contrast, was settled almost

To make wampum, Indians cut shells of snails or clams into cylindrical beads about an eighth of an inch in diameter and about an inch long. These beads were polished and strung on threads of animal gut. Each wampum string was usually about six feet long and was called a "peague" (rhymes with league). Peagues were worked into bands from one to five inches across, which were worn on the wrist, around the waist, or over the shoulder.

"Providence" means God's direction, which Williams believed he was following in coming to Rhode Island.

by accident. Williams, a lone man searching for refuge, fled into the wilderness. When other people followed him, a settlement was born. It grew fast, however, as Williams bought more land and settlers founded new communities.

There were other differences, too. Williams made it easy for settlers to farm the land, assigning equal shares to each of 12 fellow heads of households for what amounted to a few dollars. The town government in Providence was also more democratic than in any other early colony, with all male heads of households having an equal voice. And, in stark contrast to other colonies, religious freedom was practiced from the settlement's earliest days.

Even as the first colonists were busily building their homes in Providence, religious unrest continued in the Bay Colony, and dissenters arrived in Providence regularly. One of the most outspoken was Anne Hutchinson, who came in March 1638. Williams suggested that Hutchinson and her followers establish a colony on Aquidneck, a large island in Narragansett Bay, and he helped them purchase the land from the Indians. On that island, Hutchinson's group founded Portsmouth. The next year, William Coddington left Portsmouth over political conflicts and established Newport at the other end of Aquidneck Island.

Rhode Island already had its share of unrest. An unpredictable fanatic named Samuel Gorton caused so much trouble in Portsmouth that he was finally banished from the town. After moving to Providence, he spent 20 months stirring up conflicts

"There goes many a ship to sea. . . . It hath fallen out sometimes that both Papists [Catholics] and Protestants, Jews and Turks may be embarked in one ship. . . . All that I ever pleaded for . . . [was] that none of the Papists, Protestants, Jews or Turks be forced to come to the ship's prayers or worship, if they practice any. . . . The commander of the ship ought to command the ship's course . . . and also command that justice, peace, and sobriety be kept and practiced, both among the seamen and the passengers."
—Williams, comparing the government to a ship at sea, 1655

there, arguing with the civil authorities and demanding his rights as an English citizen. His followers made bizarre interpretations of the Bible that raised concerns as far away as the Massachusetts Bay Colony. In 1643, Gorton left Providence to found a settlement that came to be known as Warwick.

Not long after Williams fled Massachusetts to found his colony, the Pequot Indians began to wage

The Pequot War

The Pequot war had its beginnings in several tragic events. In 1633, three years before Williams founded Providence, the Pequots or their allies killed Captain John Stone, a Virginia trader of questionable character. Then, in 1634, they murdered another trader, John Oldham of the Bay Colony, also known as a troublemaker.

The English responded with rampant plunderings of Pequot villages on Block Island and near the mouth of the Connecticut River. In retaliation, the Pequots attacked small settlements in Connecticut in 1635 and 1636, killing about two dozen settlers.

In May 1637, the settlers of New England sent soldiers to attack the Pequot village near present-day Saybrook, Connecticut. In addition to soldiers under the command of Captain John Underhill

of the Bay Colony and Captain John Mason of Connecticut, several hundred Indian allies took part in the action. A massacre followed. Soldiers set fire to the village, and in minutes the huts housing about 800 Indians were ablaze. Indians fled from the burning village only to meet death at the hands of the Englishmen. Hundreds of women and children died in the fire. Following this massacre, the few surviving Pequots were relentlessly pursued and killed or sold into slavery, until the tribe was largely destroyed.

This 1637 drawing of the massacre of the Pequots shows how Captain Underhill and Captain Mason overpowered the Indians' bows and arrows with their guns and broke through the palisade defenses on opposite sides to destroy the village.

a war against colonists in Connecticut. In 1636, Pequot messengers asked the Narragansett chiefs Canonicus and Miantunomi to form an alliance with them to wage war against the English colonies. Massachusetts officials—the same leaders who had banished Williams—now asked his help in preventing the alliance. Williams hurried from Providence to Canonicus's village across the bay. There he met

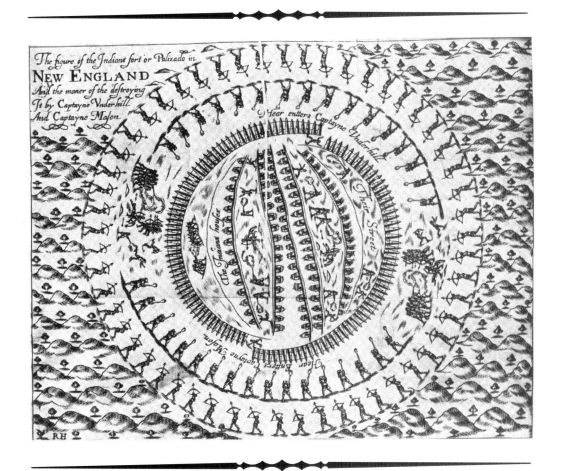

with the Narragansetts and convinced them to side with the English. The Pequots did end up in a bloody war with the settlers, but they fought without the help of the Narragansetts. If the Narragansetts had joined the Pequots, the war would have been even more destructive.

At first, the four communities of Providence, Portsmouth, Newport, and Warwick were not joined as a single colony. Williams knew, however, that if Rhode Island was to survive, the towns would have to band together. By 1643, the Massachusetts Bay Colony and Plymouth were both pressing claims to Rhode Island territory. At the same time, the threat of Indian attack was always real, no matter how good relations between Williams and the Narragansetts and other tribes might appear. The only way to protect the colony was to receive a charter from the king establishing Rhode Island as a united colony. In March 1643, Williams sailed for England. He obtained a charter the next year uniting the four towns as Providence Plantations.

While he was in England, Williams wrote several pamphlets explaining his evolving religious beliefs. In these pamphlets, he argued that all people were entitled to religious liberty. He also contended that a government is created by its people and should not wield power that is not given to it by the people. These ideas, now at the center of the American way of life, were virtually unheard of in those days. Williams took religious liberty to heart—by 1639, he had left all established churches and worshipped alone.

Peace with the Narragansetts depended on Williams's friendships with Miantunomi and Canonicus. Miantunomi was murdered under mysterious circumstances in 1643, straining relations with the colonists. Canonicus, Williams later wrote, "love[d] me as his son." When he died in June 1647, the English lost a crucial ally.

Rhode Island's official name is the State of Rhode Island and Providence Plantations. This name refers to the early settlement on Aquidneck Island (later Rhode Island) and the settlements known together as the Providence Plantations.

THE

BLOVDY TENENT,

of Persecution, for caufe of
Conscience, difcuffed, in

A Conference *betweene*

TRVTH and PEACE.

VV H O,

In all tender Affection, prefent to the High
Court of *Parliament*, (as the *Refult* of their
Difcourfe) thefe, (amongft other *Paffages*)
of *higheft confideration*.

Printed in the Year 1644.

*The title page of Roger
Williams's 1644 book,* The
Bloody Tenent of
Persecution. *Because God's
ways cannot be known, wrote
Williams, no one should be
prevented from following the
dictates of conscience.*

Dissension in the colony continued even after
Williams received his charter from King Charles I.
William Coddington, the one-time follower of Anne
Hutchinson and founder of Newport, was an ambi-
tious man who dreamed of having his own colony on
Aquidneck Island. To this end, he managed to delay
the union of the four settlements until 1647. Four
years later, Coddington stirred up more trouble and
challenged the union when he obtained a commission that split the colony in two and made him the

governor of Aquidneck for life. To answer this challenge, Williams sailed again to England where, in 1652, he got Coddington's commission rescinded.

When he returned to Rhode Island in 1654, Williams worked to make the four towns a single colony. In September of that year, he was elected to the first of three one-year terms as president of the General Court, as the government of Providence Plantations was known. It took two years, but the colony was solidly united by 1656. During this period, the first Jews came to Rhode Island, as did the first Quakers. Feared, hated and persecuted in other colonies—including the Massachusetts Bay Colony—members of both these groups were left at peace in Rhode Island. Thanks to the ideals of religious tolerance that were made part of the colony's foundation, Newport later became home to the first synagogue (Jewish house of worship) built in America.

Williams chose not to seek another term in office in the summer of 1657, but he continued serving the colony he had founded, most significantly by getting a new charter from King Charles II in 1663. Throughout his life, Williams sought the truth that would lead to his salvation by God. About three years after he founded Providence, he started the first Baptist church in America. Not long after this, he became what was known as a "seeker." This meant he was not the member of any organized church. Instead, he searched alone for God's truth.

In 1675, when Williams was about 72 years old, he experienced what must have been one of his

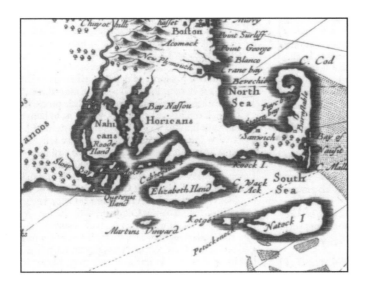

King Philip was murdered in April 1676, ending the most destructive war in American history. One of every 10 Englishmen in New England was captured or killed. The Indians suffered even more. Hundreds were killed or enslaved, and their resistance to the spread of colonization was wiped out.

greatest disappointments. That year, Williams's old friends the Narragansetts joined together with the Wampanoags when Massasoit's son, Metacomet (known as King Philip), waged war against the English. Williams reluctantly took part in the war as one of two commanders of a small army sent from Providence. Both Indians and colonists committed acts of great cruelty in the bloody war. The elderly Williams witnessed the destruction of Providence and Warwick. He was also saddened to see the once powerful Narragansetts enslaved after their defeat.

Roger Williams lived for about a half-dozen years after King Philip's War. He died sometime between January 16 and March 15, 1683. His legacy is perhaps more than anything a legacy of free thinking. As Williams wrote in 1652, "In the poor small span of my life, I desired to have been a diligent and constant observer."

Slavery in the Northeast

Rhode Island may have been a haven for religious freedom, but it was not a land of freedom. The North American slave trade became centered in Rhode Island in the eighteenth century.

Two centuries earlier, Europeans establishing colonies in the New World sought slaves to labor in mines and on plantations. Portuguese ships exploring the coast of West Africa began to trade weapons, cloth, and whiskey for human beings.

The first blacks to arrive in America came ashore at Jamestown, Virginia, in 1619. These people came as servants, but the status of Africans declined into slavery within a few decades. Slavery was not restricted to the southern colonies. It is thought that slaves from Africa arrived in

Africans were sold to the Europeans by other Africans. Slaves were usually captured by rival tribes in raids and were then bound together and marched to the coast.

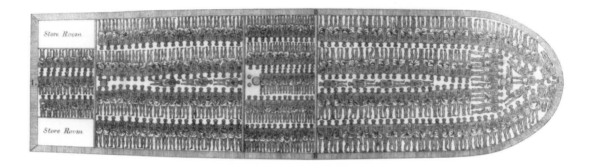

This cross section shows captives stowed on a slave ship. There were 292 people crowded into this deck, with an additional 130 on shelves above. Epidemics spread quickly in these conditions.

New Netherland as early as 1630, and slaves were used throughout the Northeast. The first colony to make slavery legal was not in the South. The Massachusetts Bay Colony put slavery in its 1641 code of laws.

Northeasterners had tried to enslave Indians, but black slaves quickly replaced Indians because many Indians died of European diseases. Other Indian slaves escaped into the familiar countryside.

As southern colonies developed an agricultural economy, the demand for slaves increased in the South. This led to what was known as the "triangular trade," a system that helped make many colonists in northeastern colonies like Rhode Island—even people who didn't own slaves themselves—wealthy as slave traders.

Here's how the triangular trade worked: Ships would leave England with trade goods and stop at the west coast of Africa. There they would barter their merchandise for Africans captured by enemy tribes and sold to coastal traders. After sailing across the Atlantic on a voyage that saw all but the healthiest slaves die, the ships called at the West Indies. At this point, the surviving slaves were traded for sugar or molasses. Ships would then dock at ports in New England, where these products were needed to make rum. The return voyage to England with a valuable cargo of rum or New England timber completed the triangle.

Of course, none of this lucrative business was possible without African slaves. Black men, women, and children became a source of great wealth to many merchants, ship owners, and shipbuilders in the Northeast.

Chapter Five

Anne Hutchinson
and the
Spread of Puritan Dissidents

On a September day in 1634, a ship called the *Griffin* docked in Boston's busy harbor after a long and arduous voyage from England to the Massachusetts Bay Colony. One of about 200 passengers on board was Anne Hutchinson, a woman destined to become one of the most famous early settlers in America and the founder of the city of Portsmouth, Rhode Island.

Anne Marbury Hutchinson was born in July 1591 in Lincolnshire in northeastern England. Her father, Francis Marbury, was an Anglican clergyman in the town of Alford. Anne's mother, Bridget, was Francis Marbury's second wife. The Marbury family was large. Young Anne had 3 older sisters (2 born to Francis's first wife). Eleven more boys and girls were born after her.

Sculptor Cyrus E. Dallin created this statue of Anne Hutchinson for the Massachusetts State House in 1915. By that time, the woman driven from the Massachusetts Bay Colony as a heretic had become an American hero.

Ocean passages on crowded, slow-moving vessels were hazardous. Passengers faced not only pirates and storms at sea, but also the threat of illness and starvation. Scurvy, a deadly disease caused by a lack of vitamin C, killed many ocean passengers. Other diseases were caused by the rats that flourished on board ship.

Hutchinson later described the eight-week voyage across the Atlantic as difficult and dangerous. Sharks followed the *Griffin* for part of the voyage and a pirate ship once threatened, only to turn tail at the sight of the ship's guns. The discomfort of the voyage was made worse by the presence of 100 cattle ordered by the Massachusetts Bay Colony. While packed in with the 200 other passengers on the vessel, Hutchinson held religious meetings with other women passengers. She also made statements about her belief in direct revelations from God, raising suspicions among some of her shipmates.

Two of Anne Hutchinson's fellow passengers reported this unorthodox belief to church leaders after their arrival in Massachusetts. As a result, Hutchinson's acceptance into the Boston church was delayed, but she was finally approved after undergoing an interrogation by three ministers. The family moved into a large house, and William and Anne dived into life in Boston. Thanks to her sharp mind and her willingness to be of service to her neighbors, Hutchinson quickly became a favorite with many of the settlers. In the colony, as in England, she helped women during childbirth and also treated the sick children of Native American women who had heard about her skills as a healer.

In addition to providing medical care to the women of the colony, Hutchinson spoke with them about her religious views, particularly her belief that good deeds and moral behavior did not prove a person was saved. She also contended that people who were saved received direct communication from

In Anne Hutchinson's time (and until the nineteenth century), infants were delivered not by doctors but by midwives. Midwives usually learned about birthing by giving birth to several children themselves and by assisting more experienced midwives when friends or relatives gave birth. Often they also provided medical care for the treatment of rashes and other minor disorders.

God. Hutchinson's teachings challenged Puritan ideas that obeying religious and civil laws—and human leaders—was a sign of a good Christian.

At first, Hutchinson spoke to just a few women meeting informally at her house. But within a few months, these informal meetings became regular gatherings of men as well as women, who came to hear Hutchinson's interpretations of the sermons

Legal-minded Puritans called Hutchinson and her followers "Antinomians" because they supposedly opposed moral law. "Nomos" is the Greek word for law.

Hutchinson preaches to a group at her home. Usually her listeners asked her questions while she, "(gravely sitting in the chair), did make answers thereunto," wrote Thomas Weld, an opponent who observed one of her meetings. Most Puritan houses had only one chair, reserved for the husband as the head of the family. To sit in the chair was a sign of importance.

delivered in church. By 1635, groups of up to 80 men and women gathered in the Hutchinson house twice weekly. One male follower insulted the local ministers by calling her "a woman who preaches better than any of your black-coats."

Although he thought she was a good midwife, Governor John Winthrop saw Hutchinson as a threat to the colony. Her ideas that salvation did not depend upon strict obedience to the laws of the church and the state were contrary to everything he held dear. If everybody believed as Hutchinson did, he feared, the colony would be torn apart.

Events soon showed that Winthrop's concerns were justified. Within two years of Hutchinson's arrival, the Bay Colony was divided. Henry Vane, a wealthy young nobleman who was elected governor in 1636, supported Anne Hutchinson. So did her old friend John Cotton and a majority of Boston citizens. A smaller group backed Winthrop and the Reverend John Wilson, the pastor of the church in Boston. Wilson felt threatened by Hutchinson. In October 1636, she led a group of Boston church members demanding that John Wheelwright be named second teacher in the church.

For a time, Winthrop was unable to put a stop to Hutchinson's teachings. Then, in May 1637, Vane and several other Hutchinson backers were voted out of office. Winthrop was named governor once again, with his followers as assistants.

As governor, Winthrop could take action against Hutchinson and her supporters. In August, he convened a meeting, or synod, of the colony's church leaders to deal with the Antinomians. After nine days of arguments and discussions, the synod found that 82 of the opinions held by Hutchinson and her followers were wrong or even blasphemous. In addition, it found that large meetings led by a

"As soon as [Hutchinson] was admitted into the church, she began to go to work, and being a woman very helpful in times of childbirth and other occasions of bodily infirmities, and well furnished for means of those purposes, she easily insinuated herself into the affections of many."
—John Winthrop

Sir Henry Vane (1613-1662) left Massachusetts shortly after losing his bid for reelection. Even though Vane tried to prevent the beheading of King Charles I by the Puritans in 1649, he was executed for treason in 1662, two years after the monarchy was restored.

woman were "disorderly, and without rule." The civil authorities demanded that Hutchinson appear before the General Court to answer charges that she was destroying the stability of the colony.

Anne Hutchinson continued to hold meetings for the next three months, but in November she appeared before the General Court in Newtown (now Cambridge) that would determine her future. The court also was to pass sentence on her brother-in-law John Wheelwright, a minister who, like Hutchinson, held heretical opinions. Other colonists identified as Antinomians also faced trial.

One after another, men who supported John Wheelwright and Anne Hutchinson were stripped of their offices and voting rights. One was banished from the colony. Next, Wheelwright himself was ordered to leave. Then it was Hutchinson's turn.

For two days, Hutchinson was forced to stand in the town meeting house as she answered one charge after another. She argued brilliantly, quoting from the Scripture to prove her right to instruct women. It appeared that she would emerge from her trial victorious. Had she kept quiet at this point, she probably would have escaped with no more than a scolding. Suddenly, however, Hutchinson told Winthrop and the other judges a revelation. She claimed God had revealed to her that she would be persecuted in the Bay Colony. But, she continued, God would allow no harm to come to her.

"Take heed how you proceed against me," she warned, "for I know that for this . . . God will ruin you and your posterity, and this whole state."

"Mrs. Hutchinson, you are called here as one of those that have troubled the peace of the common-wealth and the churches here: you are known to be a woman that hath had a great share in the promoting and divulging of those opinions that are the cause of this trouble . . . and you have maintained a meeting and an assembly in your house that hath been condemned by the general assembly as a thing not tolerable nor . . . fitting for your sex. Therefore, we have thought good to send for you to understand how things are, that if you be in an erroneous way we may reduce you [convince you of your errors] so you may become a profitable member here among us; otherwise . . . then the court may take such course that you may trouble us no further."
—John Winthrop's opening statement at Anne Hutchinson's trial

How, the judges asked, did she know that she was receiving a message from God and not the devil?

Because God himself had spoken directly to her, she answered.

This, to the Puritan mind, was heresy. Her claim was so evil that she had to be punished. Of the 49 men questioning Hutchinson, only a few, including John Cotton, still supported her. When asked by the court if it were possible that Hutchinson's revelations came from God, Cotton remarked that she might "have some special providence of God to help her is a thing that I cannot bear witness against."

But Anne Hutchinson's fate was sealed. When Winthrop called for a vote, all but three of the ministers and officials in the meeting house raised their hands, signaling that Hutchinson must be punished. Apparently afraid to link his future any further with hers, Cotton also voted in the majority. Winthrop quickly pronounced the punishment to her. "Mrs. Hutchinson, the sentence of the court you hear is that you are banished from out of our jurisdiction as being a woman not fit for our society."

Still, Hutchinson did not give up. "I desire to know wherefore [why] I am banished," she said.

"Say no more," Winthrop roared. "The court knows wherefore and is satisfied."

For the next several months, Hutchinson—pregnant for the sixteenth time (her fifteenth child, a son named Zuriel, had been born in March 1636)—lived under house arrest in the nearby town of Roxbury. Hutchinson was 46, and her pregnancy took a toll on her as she waited for spring before

"She did much good in our town, in woman's meeting[s] and at childbirth travails, wherein she was not only skillful and helpful, but readily fell into good discourse with the women."
—John Cotton,
at Hutchinson's trial

The site of the brand-new Harvard College was chosen at the meeting banishing Hutchinson. It was built in Newtown even though Boston was the larger town because Newtown was free of the Antinomian problem.

Through all this turmoil, Governor Winthrop must have been a forbidding presence, for his house was just across the street from the home of Anne Hutchinson.

After Hutchinson was exiled, her followers were ordered to surrender their weapons and ammunition because the Massachusetts Bay Colony feared an armed insurrection.

leaving. And her troubles were not yet over. Fearing Hutchinson might lead other women astray, the Boston church summoned her on March 22, 1638. Church members excommunicated her (forced her to leave the church) because of her beliefs.

Hutchinson and her children left several days after she was excommunicated. For six days, they journeyed by canoe and on foot to the settlement founded by Roger Williams just a few years earlier. There Hutchinson was reunited with her husband, who had come several weeks before. Her journey must have been hard, for the ground was still snow covered and she was well into a difficult pregnancy.

Sadly, Hutchinson miscarried the baby not long after her arrival in Rhode Island. She and her family stayed in Providence as she recovered. They were soon joined by about 18 other followers, several of whom had been excommunicated for protesting Hutchinson's treatment. Soon, Hutchinson and her friends moved to Aquidneck Island in Narragansett Bay (now, like the state, called Rhode Island). While William built a simple frame house, the family lived in a pit dug in the ground, with a plank floor and earthen walls covered with tree bark.

Several months after the Hutchinsons moved to Rhode Island, Hutchinson was nearly killed in an earthquake. Hearing of the quake, John Winthrop wrote that it proved "God's continued disquietude against the existence of Anne Hutchinson." Both Winthrop and Cotton seemed to find pleasure in her troubles. Cotton, her former friend and mentor, said her miscarriage "might signify" the errors of her beliefs. Governor Winthrop repeated to anyone who would listen the tale of how the heretic lost her baby.

But Hutchinson was unstoppable. Once she and her family were settled in, she began preaching again. Not content to have her out of Massachusetts, Winthrop now sent three ministers to convince her of the error of her ways. Hutchinson responded angrily, charging that the Boston church was "no church of Christ." At the same time, the ministers tried to convince William to denounce his wife's teachings. William, who was devoted to Anne, told the ministers from Boston that he cared more for his wife than he did for the church. In any case, he declared, she was "a dear saint and servant of God."

The Bay Colony, meanwhile, was growing less tolerant. Non-Puritans who came to Boston could face punishments of mutilation or even execution.

John Winthrop's views did not change. After Hutchinson's banishment, he described a case of a woman supposedly driven insane by reading and writing too much. "If she had attended her household affairs, and such things as belong to women," he said, "and not gone out of her way and calling to meddle in such things as are proper for men, whose minds are stronger, etc. she had kept her wits, and might have improved them usefully and honorably in the place God had set her."

Mary Dyer

Mary Dyer, one of Hutchinson's followers, was born in England in 1610 and emigrated to Boston with her husband, William, in 1635. In the midst of Hutchinson's troubles in 1637, Dyer, who was seven months pregnant, went into labor. Hutchinson and another midwife named Jane Hawkins rushed to her side. After hours of labor, Dyer delivered a deformed, stillborn child.

The Puritans believed a "monster" birth was a sign of God's displeasure. Not wanting anybody to see the dead child, Hawkins and Hutchinson buried it in the woods. Unfortunately, they were spotted by a man who revealed the event after Hutchinson left the colony. Winthrop—and doubtless many others—found this convincing evidence of Hutchinson's evil.

Mary Dyer and her family followed Hutchinson to Rhode Island. In 1650, Dyer returned to England, where she became a Quaker. Six years later, Dyer came back to America, planning to make her way to Rhode Island. By this time, hatred of Quakers in the Bay Colony was at a fever pitch. While in Boston, Dyer was arrested, stripped to the waist, and whipped in public because of her religious beliefs. A brave woman, she refused to accept the intolerance and repression in the Puritan colonies. Over the next several years, she continually challenged the Massachusetts authorities instead of fleeing to Rhode Island. In 1660, she was hanged.

As Mary Dyer stood on the top of a ladder with a rope around her neck, ready to die, she called out, "My life not availeth me in comparison to the liberty of the truth!" She wanted to say more, but her voice was stopped as the executioner pulled the ladder from beneath her feet and her body dropped.

Executions in the Massachusetts Bay Colony were public spectacles designed to prevent crime by displaying the terrible fate of the criminal. Officials warned the crowd about the dangers of crime, and ministers exhorted the prisoner to repent before death.

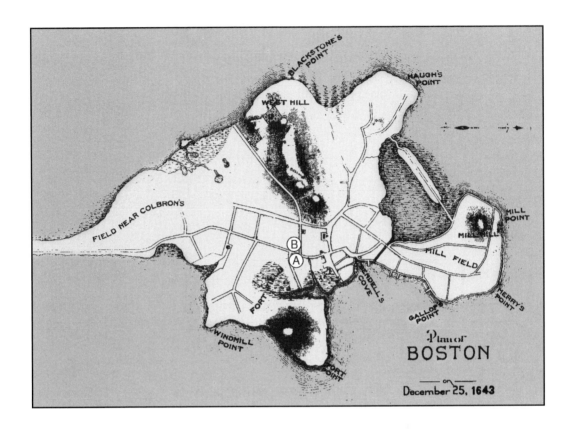

Plan of
BOSTON
December 25, 1643

Puritans who spoke openly of unorthodox ideas were excommunicated and banished as Hutchinson had been. Many came to Portsmouth, where they found Hutchinson leading the settlement.

All this changed in the spring of 1642, when William Hutchinson, Anne's husband of 31 years, died. Soon after his death, ministers from the Bay Colony visited Hutchinson and her followers. The ministers told Hutchinson the Bay Colony was going to assume control of both Portsmouth and Exeter, New Hampshire, where Hutchinson's brother-in-law John Wheelwright had started his settlement.

Boston in 1643 was as harsh a place as ever for rebels. Some of the Hutchinson children, however, had stayed. Governor John Winthrop lived just northeast of Fort Field (A). Across the street, Edward Hutchinson still lived in his parents' old house (B).

The visiting ministers urged Hutchinson to recant. Instead, she decided to move yet again—far enough from the Bay Colony this time to escape the long arm of Winthrop and the other Massachusetts leaders. After considering some land near present-day Ossining in New York, Hutchinson and six of her children settled in a vacant house on Long Island, overlooking Pelham Bay. Settlers living nearby were disturbed that Hutchinson would not keep firearms in her house. The Siwanoy Indians, they warned, were angered by the presence of the Europeans. Hutchinson, however, said she had long had friendly relations with the Indians and had nothing to fear. She was wrong.

In August or September of 1643, an Indian named Wampage and a small band of warriors attacked the Hutchinson house. Hutchinson was at home with six of her children, a son-in-law, and several servants. In minutes, everyone in the house except Susanna, the youngest child, was dead.

Anne Hutchinson's contributions as one of the founders of the northeastern frontier go far beyond the settlement of Portsmouth, Rhode Island. Her banishment from the Bay Colony prompted many in the colony to question authority and reconsider their religious beliefs.

Today, a statue of Anne Hutchinson stands in front of the Massachusetts State House in Boston—the city from which she was banished in 1638. A marker at the First Church of Boston pays tribute to her with the words: "Anne the Pioneer, Anne the Trouble-Maker, Anne the Martyr."

Hutchinson's daughter Susanna was about 10 at the time of the Indian attack in which her family members were killed. Wampage took her back to the tribe. In 1647, four years after her capture, Susanna was released from captivity when friends of her family paid a ransom. At the time of her release, she said she was sad to leave the Siwanoys, who had adopted her into the tribe.

"I never heard that the Indians in those parts did ever before commit the like outrage upon any one family or families; and therefore God's hand is . . . seen herein, to make her and those belonging to her an unheard of heavy example of their cruelty."
—Puritan preacher Thomas Weld

Rhode Island: From Settlements to Statehood

By the time of Roger Williams's death in 1683, Rhode Island had been a center of religious freedom for nearly three decades, thanks in part to the charter granted by King Charles II. Rhode Island also grew prosperous. The settlements founded by

King Charles II (1630-1685) was tolerant on religious issues because he leaned toward—and eventually converted to—Roman Catholicism, which was a persecuted religion in England during his time.

Williams, Hutchinson, and other exiles from the Bay Colony increased in size, and rich farm lands enabled the colonists to produce agricultural products, including wool, meat, and cheese for trade with the West Indies, Europe, and the Far East.

When the English government began to tax the thriving colony, conflicts between Rhode Islanders and the British became common. England responded in 1772 by sending ships to guard Rhode Island's harbors and collect taxes. In June of that year, furious colonists attacked and burned the British cutter *Gaspee*. These seeds of rebellion flowered four years later when Rhode Island declared its independence from England on May 4, 1776, even before the Declaration of Independence was signed.

During the Revolutionary War, Rhode Islanders fought in every battle and Rhode Island native Nathaniel Greene served as George Washington's second-in-command. Despite the colony's patriotism, Newport was occupied by British troops for almost three years, and 5,000 residents fled as the British destroyed much of the city.

Rhode Island was the last state to ratify the U.S. Constitution because its citizens were concerned about giving too much power to the federal government. In 1790, however, Rhode Island became the thirteenth state in the Union.

Chapter Six

Thomas Hooker
and the
Founding of Connecticut

O n a spring day in 1633, two Puritan preachers were talking together in a house in
Towcester in central England. One was Thomas
Hooker. The second was Hooker's friend, Samuel
Stone. After meeting earlier in the day, the two men
had returned to Stone's house. As they spoke, they
probably kept their voices low, for Hooker was a
wanted man. He was hiding from agents of William
Laud, the head of the Anglican Church. Laud was
imprisoning Puritan preachers because of their
beliefs.

Suddenly, there was a loud knock at the door.
Looming in the doorway, one of Laud's magistrates
asked Stone where Hooker was.

As a God-fearing Puritan, Stone wanted to
answer truthfully. He also wanted to protect his

*Thomas Hooker (1586-1647)
moved his whole congregation
to Connecticut in search of
better land and some peace
and quiet.*

Crowning his career as defender of the Church of England, William Laud (1573-1645) rose to be archbishop of Canterbury in 1633. This position gave him increased power to stamp out Puritans and enforce strict adherence to the rituals of the Anglican Church.

friend. Thinking quickly, he found a way to do both. "I saw him about an hour ago," he answered, and mentioned a place in town. "You had best hasten thither." The officer believed Stone and went away.

Thanks to Stone's quick wit, Thomas Hooker escaped from Archbishop Laud's grasp that day. If he had been captured, he almost certainly would have been thrown into prison. Given the state of English prisons in those days, he might well have died there. Instead, he slipped away from England in 1633 and made his way to North America. In the New World, he found lasting fame as a great Puritan leader and as the founder of the first major settlement in the colony that became Connecticut.

Only bits and pieces of Hooker's early life are known for certain. It is thought that he was born in July 1586 in Leicestershire, north of London. His father, also named Thomas, was an overseer on an estate near the village of Marfield. Thomas Jr. had a brother named John and at least two sisters.

At about the age of 8, Thomas started school, probably at a grammar school in the village of Market Bosworth. He graduated when he was about 16. It is thought that he spent the next two years teaching younger boys the lessons in reading, penmanship, Latin, and religion he had just learned. In 1604, when he was about 18, Thomas enrolled at Cambridge University. His university education was paid for with a scholarship given each year to a boy who had attended the Market Bosworth school.

In those years, Cambridge University was a hotbed of Puritan activity. Its graduates included

Roger Williams, the founder of Rhode Island, and the famous Massachusetts Bay Colony preacher John Cotton. Sometime during Hooker's 14 years at Cambridge—first as an undergraduate and later as a graduate student—he became a devout Puritan.

Soon after his graduation in 1618, Hooker was ordained as a minister. As a Puritan, it was not easy for him to find a congregation. Finally, however, he found a position in Esher, a small parish in Surrey near London. There he quickly built a reputation as a powerful preacher.

In 1621, Hooker married Susannah Garbrand, the maid of a woman whom Hooker had counseled spiritually for several years. We don't know much about Susannah or their marriage except that Hooker's references to marital love in his sermons suggest that their relationship was loving and tender.

Hooker stayed at the little church in Esher until 1626, when he accepted a position to preach at the Church of St. Mary in Chelmsford, Essex, in southeastern England. At this church, word of his impassioned sermons spread even more. Meanwhile, his family was also growing. A daughter, Anne, was born about the time he and Susannah moved to Chelmsford and a second daughter, Sarah, was born the following year. Another daughter and a son, John, were born within a few years.

As Hooker became well known throughout the region, his preaching also attracted the attention of William Laud, then bishop of London. In 1629, he was ordered to appear before the bishop to answer for his nonconformity to church doctrines. At that

"The man whose heart is endeared to the woman he loves . . . dreams of her in the night, hath her in his eye and apprehension when he awakes, museth on her as he sits at the table, walks with her when he travels. . . . She lies in his bosom, and his heart trusts in her, which forceth all to confess that the stream of his affection, like a mighty current, runs with full tide and strength."
—Thomas Hooker, describing marital love in a sermon on God's love

hearing, Hooker was suspended from preaching and ordered to post a cash bond to guarantee he would return to court if he was called.

Following this hearing, Hooker returned to Essex. Out of work, he established a grammar school where he taught the sons of local families. Despite the threat posed by Laud, he also continued influencing other ministers and preaching, probably in the homes of various church members who supported his ideas.

In the midst of his troubles with Bishop Laud, Hooker's daughter Sarah died. Not long after her death, his situation grew worse. John Browning, a local Anglican minister, complained to Laud that "one Mr. Hooker, lately in question before your honour . . . doth . . . continue his former practices." It took Laud eight months to act, but Hooker was ultimately ordered to reappear before the bishop's High Commission in July 1630. Instead, Hooker went into hiding, hoping to escape England. He had gotten off easy the first time he had come before Laud. Now he would almost certainly have faced imprisonment.

For a time, Hooker hid out in England. Then, in early 1631, he and his family sailed for Holland, where the Separatist Pilgrims had found refuge more than 20 years earlier.

Hooker remained an exile in Amsterdam for about two years. While there, he became embroiled in controversies within the Puritan congregations in Holland. Like most Puritan controversies, these were complicated matters having to do with issues we would probably find unimportant today. For example, Hooker's belief that it was not sinful for a Puritan to pray with a Separatist caused him no end of grief with other Puritan leaders in Holland. But his most troublesome view was that congregations should be able to choose their own ministers without receiving the authorization of church hierarchy. Finally, Hooker gave up on the idea of staying in Holland. He knew that to preach in peace, he would have to emigrate to New England, where this concept of congregationalism was practiced.

In the spring of 1633, Hooker and his family returned to England to board a ship for America. After hiding out with Samuel Stone for a time, they boarded the *Griffin*, bound for Boston. Also on the ship that early July day were Stone and John Cotton, who would become a renowned minister in Boston. After a voyage of about two months, the *Griffin* reached port.

Shortly after landing, Hooker and Stone and their families went to Newtown (now Cambridge), where a church had been established by Hooker's followers in anticipation of his arrival. Not long after the Hooker family settled into their new home, Susannah gave birth to another son, Samuel.

In Newtown, Hooker found a tidy, if small, community. The town boasted houses with slate or board roofs and a large fenced common area where cattle grazed. On an October afternoon about five weeks after his arrival in the Bay Colony, Hooker was made pastor of the town church. Stone, his friend and protégé, was made teacher.

When Hooker, Cotton, and Stone landed in the Bay Colony, Cotton Mather later punned, God had taken care of three great needs. Colonists had "Cotton for their clothing, Hooker for their fishing, and Stone for their building."

The pastor and teacher of a Puritan church were equal in authority. The pastor's preaching would open churchgoers' hearts and minds to the beliefs of the church. It was the teacher's job to explain and define those doctrines.

Cotton Mather (1663-1728), pictured above, was Hooker's first biographer. He gave this example of the power of Hooker's preaching: A man went to Hooker's church to make fun of the sermon, but he "had not been long in the church, before the quick and powerful word of God, in the mouth of His faithful Hooker, pierced the soul of him, he came out with an awakened . . . soul, and . . . he arrived at a true conversion."

All Hooker wanted was to serve as a pastor to his flock and use his sermons to inspire people to do good. About a year after he arrived in the Bay Colony, however, he was again embroiled in controversy. John Endecott, the founder of Salem, defaced the colony's English flag by ripping out the cross that was part of its design because he considered the cross a symbol of the hated Roman Catholic Church. Although many in Massachusetts agreed with Endecott, the Puritan leaders were terrified that if the authorities in England got word of Endecott's action, they would send a royal governor to rule the colony. Hooker eventually managed to convince Endecott and his supporters that even if the cross was distasteful to Puritans, its use in the flag was not sinful. Both sides were, if not happy, at least willing to end their dispute.

In October 1635, just two months after the Endecott matter had been finally settled, Hooker found himself in the center of the crisis surrounding his friend Roger Williams. When Williams was called before the General Court to answer for his dangerous opinions, Hooker was chosen to try to get Williams to see the error of his beliefs. In a debate before the court, Hooker was unable to force the radical preacher to change his mind. Unwilling to be swayed, even by a minister he respected, Williams was forced to leave the colony.

In his first two years in the Bay Colony, Hooker found little peace. And peace was important to him—so important that he once wrote that while people must "follow the truth," it is also necessary to "be at peace with all men." Hooker became convinced he could only find that peace by leaving the colony as he had left England and then Holland.

Many of Hooker's followers—and probably the minister himself—were also unhappy with their land. The Newtown settlement was long and narrow, surrounded by marshes and thick woods. The settlers needed more and better land for planting and for their cattle.

The Connecticut region to the southwest of the Bay Colony beckoned. Since the territory had already been explored, the land-hungry settlers in Newtown knew land there was rich and plentiful. Indeed, by 1635, a few Dutch and English settlers and traders were already living in Connecticut. The Dutch colonists had built a fort and trading post called the House of Good Hope on the Connecticut River, and the English had already founded small settlements at Windsor and Wethersfield. Still, most of the land was empty of settlers, so Hooker and his followers decided to move.

At first, the emigrants tried to get approval from the Bay Colony's authorities to make the move. But those leaders, including John Winthrop, did not want to lose Hooker and his followers. Finally, the group decided to leave without permission. In October 1635, about 60 members of Hooker's congregation made the trek into Connecticut. Driving cattle, hogs, and horses before them, they arrived safely after a difficult journey at a place called Suckiaug. Hooker and the rest of his church remained behind, preparing to follow in the spring.

Connecticut's Early Days

The first European we know of to set foot in Connecticut was a Dutch explorer named Adriaen Block, who discovered the Connecticut River in 1614 and claimed it for Holland. At that time, the region was inhabited by about 20,000 Algonquian-speaking Indians, including the Pequots, the Mattabesecs, the Quinnipiacs, the Niantics, and the Mohegans.

It was many years before Europeans returned to settle the Connecticut territory. To establish trade with the various Algonquian-speaking American Indian tribes living along the Connecticut River, the Dutch built a small trading fort, the House of Good Hope, in 1633. This trading post, near the site of modern Hartford, was soon abandoned, although a few Dutch settlers remained.

In that same year, John Oldham of the Massachusetts Bay Colony opened an overland trail—probably an old Indian trail—that extended from Boston to Connecticut. As he explored the region around what was to become Hartford, he found fertile soil and plenty of beaver. He was soon followed by other Bay Colony settlers, who traded and explored along the Connecticut River. Word of the good land soon spread throughout the Bay Colony, and settlers who were unhappy with the marshes that lay along the coast of Massachusetts began to turn their eyes toward Connecticut.

Thomas Hooker and his congregation traveled south from Massachusetts along the Connecticut River to Suckiaug, which is marked with an "x" on the map.

On a May morning in 1636, Hooker led about 100 men, women, and children into the wilderness. The settlers drove about 160 cattle with them. Surrounded by thick forests, they walked along the trail blazed by Puritan trader John Oldham across southern Massachusetts until they reached the Connecticut River near the site of present-day Longmeadow. There they turned south along the east bank of the river until they reached Windsor.

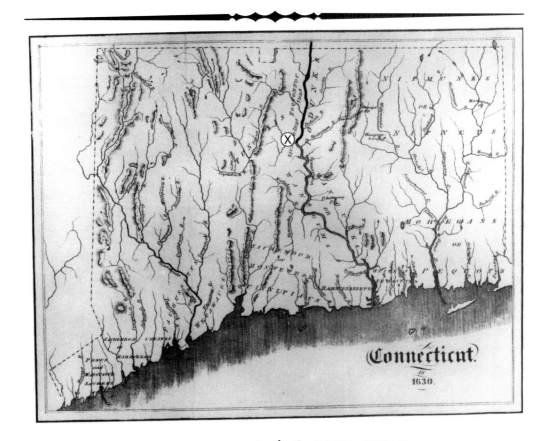

After crossing the river, they continued south to Suckiaug, where, on about June 21, they met the Puritans who had come before them. This site would become Hartford, Connecticut.

In Suckiaug, the "first comers" had already built a handful of primitive dwellings and a meeting house. Hooker and Samuel Stone were given large lots next to each other in town. Working quickly, the settlers felled trees from the plentiful forests,

Since the name Suckiaug meant "black earth," the settlers had high hopes for the land's fertility.

built wooden houses, and cleared crops for planting. Hooker's and Stone's houses overlooked the river and a large meadow.

The church in Hartford was—as churches were in every Puritan town—the center of all activities. With Hooker as pastor and Stone as teacher, services were held twice on Sunday and once at midweek. Hooker must have finally been content. For the first time since his earliest days as a minister, he could spend his time preaching instead of settling squabbles. Unlike most Puritan churches, Hooker's Hartford congregation would remain stable and harmonious throughout his tenure. He and Stone also started a school for Hartford's children.

About a year after Thomas Hooker arrived in the colony, however, the Connecticut settlements found themselves at war with the Pequot Indians. Conflicts leading to this war began when a group of Indians murdered the Connecticut pioneer John Oldham. The Bay Colony retaliated by sending a force under John Endecott, the same man who had caused so much trouble when he cut the cross from the English flag in Salem. Endecott's men terrorized Indians on Block Island, destroying whole villages. Although the Puritans in Connecticut had nothing to do with Endecott's mission, the Pequots responded by attacking Old Saybrook, Wethersfield, and other small Connecticut settlements nearby. Hartford reluctantly declared war on the Indians in the spring of 1637.

Following this war, which virtually wiped out the Pequot Indians, Hooker found himself involved

In a sermon, Hooker told soldiers leaving to fight the Pequots not to fear the Indians because "their defense is departed from them, and the Lord is with us." These soldiers later killed most of the Pequots —including women and children—in a massacre.

in the same kind of conflict he had tried to escape by leaving the Bay Colony. In August 1637, he was called to a gathering of ministers in Boston to deal with the danger presented to the Bay Colony by Anne Hutchinson. As a result of that synod, or meeting, which Hooker helped to moderate, and the trial that followed, Hutchinson was banished from the Bay Colony. Minister John Wheelwright, a Hutchinson follower, was also banished.

Life was becoming more stable in Connecticut, however. In January 1639, the villages of Hartford, Windsor, and Wethersfield joined together to form the Connecticut Colony. A fourth village, Old Saybrook, chose to stay independent. The new colony set about planning a colonial government at the meeting, using a sermon preached by Hooker the preceding spring as the inspiration. "The foundation of all authority is laid," he had declared, "in the free consent of the people." Calling for a democratic government, Hooker had stated that the "privilege of election . . . belongs to the people." These voters should also "set the bounds and limitations" on elected officials.

The Connecticut General Court also passed a series of laws based largely on these and other ideas preached by Hooker. These laws, known as the Fundamental Orders, served as Connecticut's state constitution for many years. Thomas Jefferson used ideas from the Fundamental Orders when he wrote the Declaration of Independence.

In 1643, one of Hooker's dreams came true when Connecticut, New Haven (a separate colony),

Massachusetts, and Plymouth joined together to form the Confederation of New England. Hooker had been pushing for this union of the colonies for a number of years and was the moderator at the 1643 meeting.

After the confederation was signed, Thomas Hooker turned his attention to church matters, using his 1,000-volume library to study and write about his Puritan beliefs while he continued to minister to his congregation. By 1646, he was in ill health. When a gathering of church leaders in Newtown was called that year, he could not attend. "My years and infirmities grow so fast upon me, that they wholly disenable to so long a journey," Hooker wrote to a friend.

The next year, he again had to turn down an invitation to attend a synod. His friend and fellow minister, Samuel Stone, went in his place. When Stone returned to Hartford, he found Hooker, then about 61 years old, on his deathbed. The man hailed as the founder of Connecticut died on July 7, 1647.

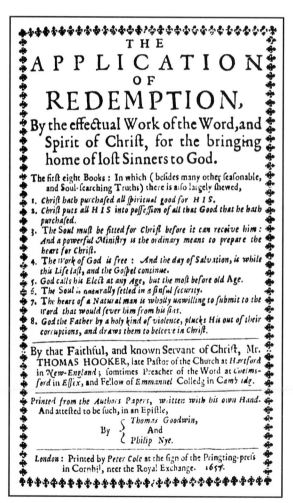

The title page of Thomas Hooker's The Application of Redemption, *which was published in two volumes a decade after the minister's death*

Connecticut: From Settlement to Statehood

In the years following Hooker's death, the government of Connecticut, established by the Fundamental Orders, expanded to include other settlements in the growing colony. Another great leader appeared in 1657, when John Winthrop Jr., the son of Massachusetts founder John Winthrop, became the governor of Connecticut. Winthrop served in that post for 18 of the next 19 years. When he took office, the colony lacked a royal charter to secure its holdings. But Winthrop traveled to England in 1662 and obtained a charter, giving Connecticut considerable self-government as well as control of New Haven Colony. Although Connecticut had continuing boundary disputes with Rhode Island, Massachusetts, and New York, the colony became similar in shape to today's state.

Between 1686 and 1688, King James II of England tried to organize all the English colonies north of Pennsylvania under one government to be known as the Dominion of New England. When his royal governor, Sir Edmund Andros, demanded that Connecticut Colony surrender its charter, the settlers resisted. The colonists are believed to have hidden the document in an oak tree in Hartford, which came to be called the Charter Oak. The threat to Connecticut's independence ended when James II was deposed in the Glorious

A plaque marks the site of the Charter Oak on Hartford's Charter Oak Avenue.

Revolution of 1688. Connecticut joined the other colonies in the Dominion of New England in ousting Andros from power and dissolving the royal government.

By the early 1700s, Connecticut farmers were producing agricultural products for sale to the other American colonies. Foreign trade was important for the colony as well, and coastal towns shipped food crops to sugar cane plantations in the West Indies.

Connecticut had a population of almost 200,000 by the 1770s. Most of these colonists favored independence from England. When the American Revolution started, about 30,000 Connecticut men volunteered for duty with the Continental army, and large amounts of food and other supplies were contributed by colonists. Connecticut native Nathan Hale, who was hanged as a spy by the British during the war, famously declared before his execution, "I only regret that I have but one life to give for my country."

On January 9, 1788, after the war's successful close, Connecticut became the fifth state to ratify the U.S. Constitution.

Captured while trying to deliver information about British positions to American forces, Nathan Hale was only 21 years old when he was hanged.

New Haven Colony

At the height of the crisis over the Antinomians in 1637, Puritans Theophilus Eaton and John Davenport arrived in the Bay Colony. A shipload of Puritan followers came with them. Eaton, a well-to-do merchant, and Davenport, a minister, thought John Winthrop and the other Puritans in Massachusetts were not sufficiently harsh in dealing with Anne Hutchinson and her followers. Desiring to live in a place in which there was strict adherence to the laws of God, in 1638 Eaton and Davenport moved to Long Island Sound, west of the Connecticut River. There, on the Connecticut coast, the two leaders founded a theocracy, a government ruled by religious leaders, which they called New Haven Colony.

The laws in New Haven were very exacting, regulating what we might consider minor details and personal decisions. For example, men were required to keep their hair cut neatly, and married couples were not allowed to separate or divorce.

In contrast to the haphazard development of other early New England towns, New Haven was neatly laid out in nine squares.

Within just a few years, other discontented settlers from the Bay Colony founded about a dozen small settlements near the city. In 1643, New Haven became the chief town of a colony that encompassed the southwestern portion of what is now the state of Connecticut. New Haven joined the Confederation of New England when that group was formed in 1643 and became part of Connecticut in 1665.

John Whelewright

Chapter Seven

John Wheelwright
and
Exeter, New Hampshire

John Wheelwright must have been intimidating as a young man. Oliver Cromwell, who would become the Puritan dictator of England and executioner of King Charles I, shook in his shoes when he played ball against the man he called "Big John Wheelwright" at Cambridge University. It is believed that John Wheelwright was born in Lincolnshire, England, in 1592. His father, Robert, and his grandfather John were farmers, hard-working men who tilled and planted their own land north of London.

Since there are no records of Wheelwright's early years, all we can do is guess what his life was like. Religion was at the heart of the typical English person's life then, so he probably spent much of his time in church. He was also strong and athletic.

This portrait of John Wheelwright (c.1592-1679) hangs in the State House in Boston. Note the spelling "Whelewright" in his signature. People chose spellings arbitrarily until spelling books and then dictionaries were introduced in the late 1700s.

The Rise and Fall of Oliver Cromwell

John Wheelwright's old classmate Oliver Cromwell, born in 1599, was a leader in Parliament of the Puritan opposition to King Charles I. In the 1640s, he became a brilliant general during the English Civil War between the Royalists defending the king and the Puritans.

After the execution of King Charles I in 1649, Cromwell became commander-in-chief of the Puritan armies fighting in Ireland and Scotland. Four years later, he was made lord protector of England, ruling almost like a king. With a Puritan as head of state and a Puritan Parliament, Puritans in England had no more reason to emigrate to North America. The rapid growth of Massachusetts came to a quick halt.

Cromwell died on September 3, 1658, and was succeeded as lord protector by his son, Richard. But Royalists brought King Charles II back to power in 1660 and the days of Puritan rule came to an end. Oliver Cromwell's body, which had been buried in Westminster Abbey, was disinterred, hanged, and beheaded by order of the new king.

John probably suffered through the more than 10 hours a day sitting in school under the eye of a harsh teacher with a ready cane.

But Wheelwright made use of his schooling. When he was about 19, the young man enrolled at Cambridge University, the same school that Thomas

Hooker and Roger Williams attended. Wheelwright was what was called a "sizar" at Cambridge, which meant some of his expenses were paid by the university in exchange for services he performed. It was during college that Wheelwright met Oliver Cromwell, who would go on to lead a Puritan revolution in England and ultimately head the English government.

Wheelwright received his undergraduate degree from Cambridge in 1615 and his Master of Arts degree in 1618. The year after his graduation, he was made a minister in the Church of England.

We don't know what Wheelwright did immediately following his ordination as a minister. His father died at about that time, so Wheelwright may have spent his days overseeing the land he had inherited. In November 1621, he married Marie Storey, the daughter of the minister at Bilsby, a small town in Lincolnshire. Seventeen months later, following the death of Marie's father, he was offered his father-in-law's position at Bilsby.

For the next nine years, Wheelwright served in the small Bilsby church. During these years, he and Marie had two children, a son who died soon after his birth and a daughter, Catharine. Marie herself died in about 1629, perhaps in childbirth.

In 1630, Wheelwright married again. His second wife was Mary Hutchinson, sister-in-law of Anne Hutchinson. Anne and William Hutchinson lived in Alford, just one mile from the Wheelwrights. In the coming years, Anne and John had a great deal of spiritual influence on each other. And they would meet similar fates at the hands of intolerant Massachusetts Bay Colony authorities.

During his years as a minister, Wheelwright also became a friend and follower of John Cotton, one of the leading Puritan ministers in England. Like Cotton, he probably wore no fancy robes when he preached to his congregation; nor did he use the cross in his services. By turning his back on these and other elements of the Anglican faith, he earned the enmity of William Laud, bishop of London. In 1632, John Wheelwright was "silenced"—ordered to preach no more. The next year, Cotton, his mentor, was forced to leave England for America.

Following Laud's ruling, Wheelwright—like Thomas Hooker—probably became a "bootleg" preacher, meeting with Puritans in private homes in Lincolnshire. If he did, he managed to keep his activities secret from William Laud, who in 1633 became archbishop of Canterbury, the most powerful church position in England. He kept them so quiet, in fact, that we're not sure just what he did in the years between his silencing and early 1636. That year, Wheelwright left England for Boston. It's safe to assume he was in contact with Cotton, who had become one of the Massachusetts Bay Colony's leaders, and with his sister-in-law Anne Hutchinson. In any event, on May 26, 1636, he and his family, which now included five children, sailed into Boston.

The Boston to which Wheelwright and his family emigrated was nothing like the big thriving city of today. In those days, the town was not much more than a rag-tag village on the Charles River.

Townspeople led hard lives, battling each day simply to survive on diets of fish, corn, game, and dairy products. The settlement's treasurer had the only brick house in town. Everyone else lived in homes made of mud-chinked sawn logs with thatched roofs.

When Wheelwright arrived in Boston, what was known as the "Antinomian Controversy" was raging in the Bay Colony. On one side in this controversy stood Bay Colony leader John Winthrop and pastor John Wilson. On the other side were the Antinomians, led by Anne Hutchinson; Henry Vane, the governor of the colony that year; and John Cotton. As was the case with most Puritan controversies, this one centered on what we would view as a minor difference in the interpretation of the Bible. These matters were of grave importance to the Puritans, however, for to be on the "wrong" side in a controversy could lead to banishment.

Because he was a friend of Hutchinson and Cotton, Wheelwright was seen as an Antinomian. When it was suggested that he be given a job as second teacher (a kind of assistant pastor) in the church in Boston, Winthrop—who was still the leader of a powerful faction in that town—vetoed the proposal. Wheelwright's appointment, he said, would "raise doubtful disputations" in the colony.

Soon, though, Wheelwright was offered the job of minister at the church in the nearby village of Mount Woolaston, now known as Quincy. While Winthrop and his followers in Boston considered Wheelwright a potential troublemaker, particularly since he supported Hutchinson, they still respected

Settlers in Boston and other early settlements used nets known as sieves to catch fish in bays and inlets.

Antinomianism is the belief that Christians do not need to observe moral laws if they are saved by God. Anne Hutchinson and other Antinomians believed that their religion did not require them to obey laws such as those enforcing church attendance. Puritan leaders like John Winthrop, on the other hand, held that all Puritans must observe such laws.

his abilities as a preacher. In mid-January of 1637, just eight months after his arrival, Wheelwright was invited to preach a sermon at a special Fast Day service in Boston. This fast had been called to heal differences of opinion in the colony and to seek God's protection in the war raging with the Pequot Indians.

In his Fast Day sermon, Wheelwright angered Winthrop and his friends by declaring that ministers who believed good works proved a person's salvation were leading their flocks to damnation. Two months later, he was hauled before the General Court, just as Roger Williams had been before him.

At that hearing, Wheelwright denied that the court's copy of his sermon was accurate, and he demanded to know who his accusers were. When the minister realized he would not get a fair hearing, he refused to answer any questions. Wheelwright was found guilty of sedition, or treason, and "contempt of the civil authority." Sentencing was delayed until the next General Court in May, when the election of the colony's governor would take place. In the meantime, Wheelwright was ordered to cease preaching. Just as he had been silenced by intolerant Anglicans in England, he was now silenced by equally intolerant Puritans in New England.

At the May General Court, Wheelwright's supporters prepared to read a petition in his favor. But members of Winthrop's faction demanded that elections be held first. In that election, John Winthrop was voted back into office, and men supporting his views were made his assistants. Henry Vane and

"So, after much debate, the court adjudged him guilty of sedition, and also of contempt, for that the court had appointed the fast as a means of reconciliation of the differences, etc. and he purposely set himself to kindle and increase them."
—John Winthrop, writing about Wheelwright's trial in his journal

other Bostonians who were willing to defend Wheelwright and Anne Hutchinson were suddenly out of office and out of power. Probably to avoid more conflict in the colony, sentencing was delayed again. Finally, on November 2, 1637, at the same court that found Anne Hutchinson guilty of holding heretical opinions, Wheelwright was sentenced to banishment and given two weeks to leave the colony.

After the sentencing, Wheelwright returned to Mount Woolaston to prepare for his departure. He turned down Roger Williams's offer of refuge in Rhode Island. Perhaps suffering badly at the

The stocks were a perpetual reminder of colonial leaders' power to control the population. Until 1641, when the Body of Liberties was adopted as the first legal code, Massachusetts courts imposed whatever punishments they pleased.

hands of authorities in both Europe and the Bay Colony made Wheelwright want to create a new colony in which he could preach as he wished. Whatever his reasons, he decided to move north of Boston. He went by boat as far as the site of present-day Portsmouth, New Hampshire. Then he traveled inland with a settler named John Clark until they reached a waterfall on the Squamscott River. There Wheelwright found a few people in a fishing village established in the 1620s by the Laconia Company, a joint-stock company.

New Hampshire's Beginnings

It is believed that the first European to view New Hampshire was an English sea captain named Martin Pring. In 1603, Pring sailed up the Piscataqua, a river that today divides the southern tip of Maine from New Hampshire. Captain John Smith visited the same area in 1614 and praised it as a place in which "nature and liberty affords us that freely which in England we want, or it costeth us dearly."

Smith's praise of the region attracted the attention of King James I of England. In 1620, the king granted a charter to the Council for New England to fund the colonization of the Northeast. This council consisted of a group of wealthy men, headed by Sir Ferdinando Gorges.

Captain John Smith (c.1580-1631) wrote about New Hampshire in his enormously influential Description of New England.

Two years later, Gorges teamed up with an investor named Captain John Mason to obtain grants of land that included a region known as the Province of Maine. The area stretched between the Merrimack and Piscataqua Rivers, north of the Massachusetts Bay Colony. To finance, populate, and administer the territory, the two formed a joint-stock company known as the Company of Laconia.

After a few years, that company was dissolved because it was losing money. Mason and Gorges split their holdings in 1629. Gorges took the northernmost parcel, today's Maine. This province remained a part of Massachusetts until 1820, when it obtained separate statehood. Mason was left as almost the sole proprietor of the rest of the holdings, an area named New Hampshire in honor of Captain Mason's home county, Hampshire, in England.

Although the Laconia Company was a failure, several of its early settlements around the mouth of the Piscataqua survived. The city of Portsmouth, originally called Strawberry Banke, was a Laconia settlement, as were Hampton and a smattering of huts known as Exeter. The region remained largely unsettled, however, until the late 1630s.

Ferdinando Gorges (c.1566-1647) and John Mason (1586-1635) split their holdings into New Hampshire and Maine.

It was winter when Wheelwright arrived at the site of what was to become the city of Exeter. Writing later about his trip, Wheelwright recalled (in the third person), "it was marvelous that he got thither at that time . . . by reason of the deep snow in which he might have perished." We don't know for sure how Wheelwright spent that first winter in the wilderness, but he probably found shelter with one of the small handful of settlers living in the area.

Wheelwright purchased a plot of land from Indians in early April 1638. The deed transferred a large tract along the Merrimack River to the minister and a half-dozen other Massachusetts settlers.

The deed for land acquired by Wheelwright in April 1638. The Indians selling the land signed the deed with drawings because they did not write. Look for Wheelwright's name at the end of the third line.

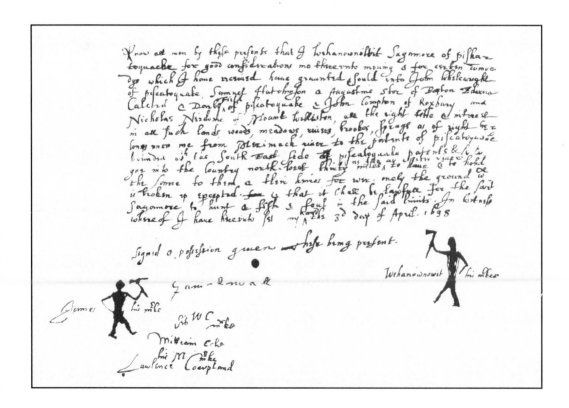

128

While these other settlers' names were included on the deed, there is no indication they had accompanied Wheelwright on his trip into the wilderness.

Wheelwright hurried to build a home, and he was joined by his wife, children, and mother-in-law just a few weeks after his arrival. Other families soon followed. Many of his friends had been punished or exiled for supporting him, and they were more than ready to be finished with the Bay Colony. By that summer, the settlement already had a church.

The next year, Wheelwright and his followers wrote what they called a "combination for self-government." This document dealt with such matters as the election of public officials, taxation, and public improvements. Included were bans on the sale of gunpowder, weapons, and liquor to Indians. It also contained a provision for trial by jury.

During the next several years, Exeter grew and flourished—at least as much as was possible in the frontier of the 1640s. By 1641, the community was large enough to support two political parties. Sadly for Wheelwright, one of these parties was in favor of making Exeter and other New Hampshire settlements part of the Bay Colony. It made sense that some in the colony might wish to join Massachusetts because the Bay Colony was the largest and most prosperous of the New England settlements. Still, it must have been difficult for Wheelwright when the citizens of Exeter petitioned the Bay Colony to absorb the settlement. He knew that if the unionists had their way, the colony would no longer be his. Worse, he knew he would have to move once again.

Life in Exeter was not easy for Wheelwright and the other early settlers. The land was harsh and rocky, and settlers lived in houses of logs daubed with mud. Even 40 years after the founding of the settlement, the most valuable possession of one of the richest men in the region was a collection of six silver spoons.

Wheelwright began looking for another place to settle. He found a refuge far to the north in a village called Wells in the province of Maine. In 1643, after the Bay Colony agreed to accept Exeter into its fold, Wheelwright and several of his followers moved to Maine.

During the next four years, Wheelwright served as pastor of a church in Wells. Although many of his parishioners were supporters who had followed him from the Bay Colony to Exeter and then to Wells, he must have been unhappy because most of the settlers in Wells were not Puritans. For the most part, they were fortune hunters who came to America simply to make money.

Several months before Wheelwright left for Maine, someone (we don't know who) asked the Bay Colony authorities to lift the ban on the preacher. Then, in April and May 1643, shortly after his move, Wheelwright wrote two letters, one to the General Court and the other to Governor John Winthrop. In those letters, he apologized for what he called his "vehement, censorious speeches," and he went on to say he wished to visit Massachusetts to "give satisfaction" to the General Court. The General Court responded quickly, giving Wheelwright permission to visit the colony for two weeks to petition for readmission. It is thought that he soon visited Boston and spoke with ministers who promised to help him get his sentence of banishment overturned.

Unfortunately, we do not know Wheelwright's motives in writing these letters. Perhaps, as he grew older, he came to think his earlier beliefs had been wrong. Or he may have simply wished to move his family to the relative safety of the Bay Colony. As the magistrates there were considering his case, Wheelwright must have been shaken to learn of the massacre of his sister-in-law Anne Hutchinson and five of her children at the hands of Indians in the late summer of 1643. In any case, Wheelwright's banishment was lifted when the Bay Colony authorities met in May 1644.

John Wheelwright had not completely caved in to the the Bay Colony's leaders, however. In his May 1643 letter to John Winthrop, the minister insisted, "I cannot with a good conscience condemn myself for such capital crimes, dangerous revelations, and gross errors, as have been charged upon me." Even while the Bay Colony authorities were considering whether to lift the minister's banishment, Wheelwright was working on *Mercurius Americanus*, a book that directly refuted Winthrop's version of the events of the Antinomian crisis. Wheelwright's book justified his views and his actions during that period.

Mercurius Americanus,
Mr. WELDS his ANTITYPE,
OR,
MASSACHUSETTS
great APOLOGIE examined,
Being *Obſervations* upon a Paper ſtyled,
A ſhort ſtory of the Riſe, Reign, and Ruine
of the *Familiſts*, *Libertines*, &c. which infected the
Churches of *NEW-ENGLAND*, &c.

Wherein ſome parties therein concerned are vindicated, and
the truth generally cleared.

By JOHN WHEELVVRIGHT junior.
φιλαλήθες.

LONDON:
Printed, and are to be ſold at the *Bull* near the Caſtle-
Tavern in Cornhill. 1 6 4 5.

Wheelwright remained in Wells for more than two years after reconciling with the Massachusetts Bay Colony, apparently waiting for a position to open up for him there. Finally, in 1647, the people of Hampton called him to work with their minister. Hampton, today a city in New Hampshire, was then considered part of the Bay Colony. In the spring of 1647, at the age of 55, the minister moved to the Puritan town and away from the rough-and-tumble village of Wells.

Wheelwright served as assistant pastor in Hampton for the next several years. His parishioners were obviously pleased with his services. In 1650, they gave him the deed to a 200-acre farm; a few years later, they increased his annual salary from 40 to 50 pounds.

In 1656, Wheelwright returned to England. The country was then under Puritan rule, and he must have felt certain he would be warmly welcomed. Perhaps the 64-year-old preacher wanted to die in his native land. If that was his wish, however, it was to be denied, for King Charles II, who had fled the Puritan Revolution, returned from exile in 1660. England was once again in the hands of the royals.

In retaliation for the English Civil War, the king now executed many Puritans. One of the victims was Henry Vane, the former governor of Massachusetts and friend of both Wheelwright and Anne Hutchinson.

Wheelwright knew he had to turn his back on England once again. Returning to America in 1662, he accepted an offer to be a minister in the town of

Salisbury, New Hampshire. He served in that post for his last 17 years. On November 15, 1679, John Wheelwright died at the age of 87.

By the time of Wheelwright's death, the Bay Colony's claims to Exeter and other settlements in New Hampshire had been denied by the English government, and New Hampshire was a royal colony. Exeter, the city founded by Wheelwright, became the colony's capital during the Revolutionary War. Today it is home to one of the most renowned preparatory schools in the world—Phillips Exeter Academy.

This map of New Hampshire was made in 1680, the year after Wheelwright's death. A small town today, Exeter (spelled "Excefter" here) was then the region's largest town.

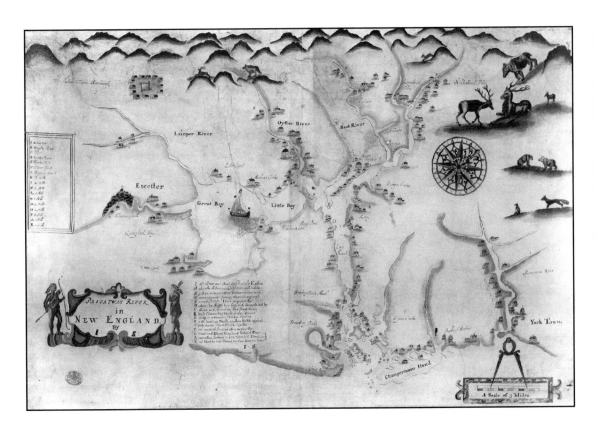

New Hampshire after Wheelwright

Land conflicts between New Hampshire and Massachusetts continued after John Wheelwright's death and both colonies granted charters to towns within the disputed area. Finally, in 1741, the British government gave New Hampshire about 3,500 square miles of disputed land and 28 towns that had been claimed by the Bay Colony. Benning Wentworth, a wealthy merchant, was named royal governor of New Hampshire.

Governor Benning Wentworth (1696-1770)

In his years as governor, Wentworth made grants for more than 100 new townships, often setting aside several hundred acres of land in each for his own use. Eventually, his landholdings grew to about 100,000 acres. In addition, he insisted that New Hampshire's territory extended west into a region that was also claimed by New York. In that area, he granted about 100 charters for townships. He named the first of these Bennington—after himself. New York, of course, complained bitterly that Wentworth was stealing its land. The dispute over the so-called "New Hampshire Grants" was resolved in 1764 in New York's favor, and the western boundary of New Hampshire was set at the western bank of the Connecticut River. In 1767, Benning Wentworth resigned from office and was succeeded by his nephew John Wentworth.

Like most colonists, New Hampshire settlers resented England's tax policies. In December 1774, an armed group attacked a fort in Portsmouth, seizing guns and powder and giving them to patriots in nearby towns. About six months later, Governor John Wentworth fled to England.

New Hampshire adopted a state constitution in January 1776, making it the first colony to declare itself independent from England. In 1788, it was the ninth state to ratify the U.S. Constitution.

Vermont: From Discovery to Statehood

Frenchman Samuel de Champlain was the first European to lay eyes on Vermont. On July 4, 1609, from a canoe traveling down the body of water we call Lake Champlain, the French explorer spied the mountains of Vermont in the distance.

Samuel de Champlain (1567-1635) was the founder of New France, the French colony in Canada.

Because of its location between the hostile British and French territories, Vermont, like Maine, was not settled for many years. The Massachusetts Bay Colony had been granted the southern half of Vermont (along with southwestern New Hampshire) in its charter. To protect its claim, the Bay Colony erected a series of forts along the Connecticut River. Fort Dummer, built in 1724 near the present town of Brattleboro, was the first permanent European settlement in what was to become Vermont.

In 1741, King George II declared that the Bay Colony's claims in present-day Vermont and New Hampshire were invalid, and he fixed the northern boundary of Massachusetts at its present location. New Hampshire's governor, Benning Wentworth, seized this chance to claim lands west of the Connecticut River in the territory that was to become Vermont. In 1749, he granted land for a town (named Bennington) in southwestern Vermont, the first of more than 100 towns. These grants were known as the "New Hampshire Grants."

Wentworth's activities upset Governor George Clinton of New York. Clinton claimed that early charters to the duke of York, for whom his colony was named, gave New York the right to the lands Wentworth was giving away. The English monarch was asked to settle the dispute, but the French and Indian War made the land conflict a low priority. In 1764, following the end of the fighting, King George III wiped out the Vermont territory by determining that the western bank of the Connecticut River was the boundary between New Hampshire and New York. As far as New York was concerned, all the so-called "New Hampshire Grants" west of the river were void. New York began to give the settled land to new colonists.

The settlers who had been granted land by Wentworth were enraged that their property was being taken, and violent outbreaks against New York authority were common. This was especially true in western Vermont, where Ethan Allen organized the Green Mountain Boys to resist the new settlers bearing New York land titles.

At the time of the Revolutionary War, the Green Mountain Boys were the only organized soldiers in the Vermont region. Under Allen's command, they turned their attention away from the land grabbers to fight the British. Their most famous exploit during the war was capturing the British fortress at Ticonderoga in 1775 with the help of Benedict Arnold.

In July 1777, citizens' representatives unanimously adopted a constitution that made what we know as Vermont an independent republic. After 14 years, Vermont decided to enter the Union as the fourteenth state on March 4, 1791.

The Green Mountain Boys were so successful at keeping New Yorkers out of their territory that they established the land as a separate republic that ultimately became the state of Vermont.

Maine: From Discovery to Statehood

One of the last northeastern regions to be settled, Maine was perhaps the first reached by Europeans. It is thought that the Vikings landed there about 500 years before Columbus sailed into the West Indies. But it took 600 more years before any European attempt at settlement was made. And that venture, by Frenchman Samuel de Champlain in 1604, lasted but a brief time. King James I of England included the region in his grant to the Plymouth Company, and another unsuccessful effort was made to settle the region in 1607 and 1608, when Jamestown was being founded in Virginia. In 1613, the French again tried to establish a settlement, a small colony on Mount Desert Island, but they were soon driven out by the English.

English attempts to settle the territory we know today as Maine began after 1622, when Ferdinando Gorges's Council for New England, as the Plymouth Company had been renamed, received a grant for the territory between the Merrimack and Kennebec Rivers. Gorges and John Mason divided the territory in 1629, with Gorges taking the portion east of the Piscataqua River. That territory was chartered in 1639 as the "Province and Countie of Maine." Because of repeated conflicts with Native American tribes, however, settlement of the region was limited. John Wheelwright entered into a truly wild area when he moved there to escape the long arm of the Massachusetts Bay Colony.

But the Massachusetts Bay Colony assumed jurisdiction of Maine in 1652, less than a decade after Wheelwright went to the region. The heirs of Gorges disputed the Bay Colony's claim until 1677, when Massachusetts purchased their proprietary rights. In 1691, a new charter was given to Massachusetts, reaffirming its control of Maine. As part of Massachusetts, Maine soon established laws and institutions much like those of the Bay Colony. Beginning in the early eighteenth century, Maine began developing prosperous fishing, shipbuilding, and lumber industries.

In 1775, when men in Boston staged the famous "tea party," the Sons of Liberty in Maine held their own tea party in York. Men from Maine were among the first to fight in the Revolutionary War. Despite this patriotism, eastern Maine was occupied by the British during much of the war.

Maine's link to Massachusetts was not cut until 1820. That year, the Missouri Compromise—a law passed by the U.S. Congress to resolve a crisis over slavery—called for Missouri to be admitted into the Union as a slave state, while Maine was admitted as a free state. Maine became the nation's 23rd state.

Chapter Eight

William Penn
and the
Quakers of Pennsylvania

I n the autumn of 1682, a tiny ship sailed west across the Atlantic Ocean. The *Welcome* was crowded. When it left England, it carried more than 100 Quaker men, women, and children fleeing religious persecution in England.

The voyage was difficult. Water and fresh food were scarce. Then, after several weeks at sea, smallpox broke out on board. Before the disease ran its course, 31 of the passengers were dead.

Throughout the voyage, the Quakers gained strength from their leader. He offered words of hope to the living even as he comforted and cared for the dying. Finally, on October 22, the settlers smelled land. As they watched shore birds soaring overhead, they knew the dangerous voyage was near its end.

William Penn (1644-1718) was a complicated man. Before adopting the humble religion of Quakerism, he was a stylish young man. And even though he was supposed to value simplicity, Penn could not stop himself from being concerned about money.

The Quakers

The Quaker religion was founded by George Fox in England in 1647. The original name for the new religion was the Society of Friends of the Truth. Quakers believed they needed no priests or ministers to understand God's messages. Instead, they received guidance through what they called an "inner light" that came from the Holy Spirit.

English people of the time considered Quakers strange and stubborn in their behavior. Quakers would not participate in the services of the Church of England, and they also refused to swear oaths or to take up arms. Since Quakers believed all people were equal, they would not remove their hats, even in the presence of royalty, and they said "thee" to everyone instead of "you" because in the seventeenth century "you" was used for superiors.

The Quakers got their name in 1650 when Fox was hauled before a judge and ordered to explain his beliefs. Fox, who often shook like a leaf when he preached, told the judge to tremble before the Lord. The judge retorted that he was a "Christian and no Quaker." The name stuck.

At their prayer meetings, Quakers would sit silent until someone felt moved to speak. The others would listen and, if similarly inspired, they would also speak in

George Fox (1624-1691) became convinced that God revealed Himself directly to Christians through an "inner light" when he had a mystical experience at age 22.

turn. Quakers believed that the words coming to people in worship were from God. As simple as their beliefs and practices were, Quakers were hated because they threatened authority and questioned customs. They were persecuted in England and in every American colony except for Rhode Island and Pennsylvania.

Six days later, the *Welcome* landed in North America. One of the first passengers to step ashore was William Penn, the Quaker who led his people from strife-torn England to a land of religious freedom in Pennsylvania.

William Penn was born on October 14, 1644, in a small house in the shadow of the Tower of London, the monarchy's private dungeon. He was the first child of William and Margaret Penn. His father was a naval officer, and his mother was the daughter of a merchant based in Holland. During much of William's childhood, his father was away at sea. For his service to England, the elder William Penn was made an admiral and knighted.

At first, young William lived in London with his mother and their servants. Then, when he was five, the family moved to a country estate about 10 miles from the city.

During William's childhood, a new religion was gaining a foothold in Europe. This religion was the Society of Friends, and its members called themselves Friends. Others referred to them as Quakers.

When William was about 13 and staying at his family's landholdings in Ireland, he heard a Quaker named Thomas Loe preach. He was enthralled by Loe's spiritual purity. During the next half-dozen years, while he studied at Oxford and traveled in France, the young man continued to be drawn to the Quakers he met. But William was also attracted by power and wealth. He dressed with style and adopted sophisticated manners—quite the opposite of the simple Quaker garb and modesty.

Penn's curiosity about the faith grew stronger in 1665 when England was devastated by the Black Plague. In the midst of the epidemic that killed about 70,000 men, women, and children, the young man saw Quakers visiting the sick and dying and offering shelter to children orphaned by the disease. Penn later said those terrible days in London gave him a "deep sense . . . of the vanity of this world, of the irreligiousness of the religions in it." Only the Quakers seemed true to their faith.

In early 1666, as the plague began to wane, Admiral Penn, perhaps trying to turn his son from his attraction to Quakerism, sent him back to Ireland. There the younger Penn oversaw the family's holdings and went to parties and dances with other wealthy English families in Ireland. He also helped to put down an Irish rebellion and briefly became fascinated by the life of a soldier. The handsome and charming man had plenty of distractions to keep from thinking about what to do with his life.

Then, in July 1667, Penn again heard Thomas Loe speak. This time he was ready for a change, and Penn formally accepted the Quaker faith that night. Although he continued to dress like a wealthy admiral's son for a time, he began to attend Quaker prayer meetings, first in Ireland and later in England. Penn was arrested for his Quaker activities just two months later, an event that made him even more devoted to his new faith. A newly modest Penn preached and wrote pamphlets defending the faith and denouncing "the vain fashionmongers of this shameless age." His preaching and writing soon got him in trouble

This portrait of a young and dashing William Penn was made the year he was in Ireland. The 22-year-old wore armor because he considered becoming a soldier.

with his father, who was infuriated that his son would accept Quakerism with its strange customs. Worse, young Penn was repeatedly arrested and jailed for violating laws enacted by King Charles II against certain religious sects.

    While Penn was locked up in the Tower of London that had loomed over his boyhood home, he wrote a book called *No Cross, No Crown*, which encouraged people to return to the simple lives of the early Christians. And he was vehement in his defiance of the king. "Those who use force in religion," he declared, "can never be in the right."

This depiction of a Quaker meeting was made by an enemy mocking the group for allowing women to speak in public. From its earliest years, Quakerism treated men and women as equals, and women served as church leaders.

Admiral Penn fell sick when his son was in prison again in 1669. While Penn knew the admiral could easily get him out of jail by paying a fine, he believed that doing so would be an admission of guilt. "I entreat thee not to purchase my liberty," he wrote to his father. The fine was paid, however, almost certainly by Admiral Penn. Ten days after his son's release, Admiral Penn died.

When Quaker founder George Fox went to America in 1671, Penn became the leader of the Quakers in Europe and traveled frequently to meet with groups in different countries. In April 1672, after a missionary trip to Holland and Germany, Penn married Gulielma Springett, a devout and intelligent Quaker woman he had known for several years. William and Guli, as she liked to be called, settled in a large house at Rickmansworth, a few hours from London by coach. Penn remained the European head of the Quakers until Fox's return to England in July 1673, but he stayed home to be close to his wife because she was frail. At Rickmansworth, Penn wrote pamphlets and political tracts defending the Quaker faith.

In the first few years of their marriage, Guli gave birth to three children, including twins, but all died as infants. Two weeks after the death of the first child, William's brother Richard also died. The Penns' house became a place of sadness. When Guli became pregnant with their fourth child, Penn took her to his mother's house. There, on January 25, 1675, Springett (named for Guli's family) was born. Following their son's birth, the family moved to

At about the time of her marriage to Penn, Gulielma Springett was, a friend remembered, "in all respects a very desirable woman, whether regard was had to her outward person, or to the endowments of her mind, which were every way extraordinary."

Wormingshurst in Sussex. During the next five years, Guli gave birth to two more children, Letitia and Billy.

While Penn was preoccupied with family concerns, the persecution of Quakers continued in England. George Fox's trip to the New World in the early 1670s had sparked the imagination of many of them. Maybe they, like the Separatists and the Puritans before them, could find a religious haven in America. Later in the 1670s, Penn himself became deeply involved in a project to found a Quaker settlement in what is now part of New Jersey. He even wrote the colony's plan of government.

In 1680, Penn realized he had a way to establish a Quaker colony. Admiral Penn had loaned King Charles II 16,000 pounds to help him regain the throne in 1660. Seeking repayment, Penn now petitioned the king to grant him a tract of land north of Maryland. On March 4, 1681, the king signed a charter giving Penn a landholding almost as large as England itself. This document made Penn the world's largest private landowner. The only cost to Penn was a payment of two beaver skins each year as well as one-fifth of all the gold and silver mined in the colony of Pennsylvania.

Penn wanted to call the land Sylvania, meaning "land of woods" in Latin. But the king insisted that the new land be called Pennsylvania to honor Penn's father. Penn later said he tried to pay a secretary 20 pounds to have the name changed since he did not want the name to be "looked on as a vanity in me, and not as a respect in the king . . . to my father."

Penn's grant was a proprietorship. This meant it was given to a single individual with the understanding that he would personally finance its settlement and upkeep, earning profits however he could. Pennsylvania was the last proprietorship in the New World.

Pennsylvania before William Penn

Before the first European ever set foot in the territory we know as Pennsylvania, the region was the home of about 15,000 Native Americans. Most were members of the Delaware, Shawnee, and Susquehanna tribes, along with some scattered groups of tribes in the Iroquois League.

The Dutch were the first Europeans to visit Pennsylvania, exploring the lands along the Delaware River in 1614. Not until 1643, however, was any attempt made to establish a European settlement. In that year, a party of Swedes claimed the territory for Sweden, calling it New Sweden and establishing two settlements near the site of what is today the city of Chester. Under the leadership of Peter Stuyvesant, the Dutch led an expedition against the Swedes and reclaimed the territory. The Dutch were forced to give up their claim in 1664 when they surrendered New Netherland to the British.

"I have a great Love and Regard towards you, and I desire to win and gain your Love and Friendship."
—Penn's message to the Indians of Pennsylvania

Penn was—for all practical purposes—the sovereign ruler of 45,000 square miles of land rich with natural resources and ideal for farming. Penn did not, however, consider himself the owner of this land. Sending a message to Pennsylvania's Indians, the true owners of the land, he pledged love and brotherhood. Penn promised to pay the Indians for all the land his colony used and to defend their rights as he would the rights of Englishmen.

With the charter in hand, Penn began organizing what he called the "Holy Experiment"—the settlement of Pennsylvania as a land where Quakers and others could live freely. He quickly assured the 2,000 or so Swedish and Dutch settlers already on the land that they would be welcome members of the new colony. At yearly rents of mere pennies, land was easily available to settlers. Penn sold 5,000-acre estates for just 100 pounds. Soon about 250 settlers were ready to move across the Atlantic.

Within just a few months after Penn received his charter, a small group of colonists, known as the "First Adventurers," was sent to the new country of Pennsylvania. Thomas Holme, a surveyor, set to work laying out Penn's plan for a great city with a regular grid of streets and plenty of green space.

The plan for Philadelphia (the rectangular grid) and surrounding lands in 1681. Penn's manor, called Springettsberry here after Guli's family name, was just north of Philadelphia. Other farming plots of varying sizes were divided for colonists. The entire area is now inside Philadelphia city limits.

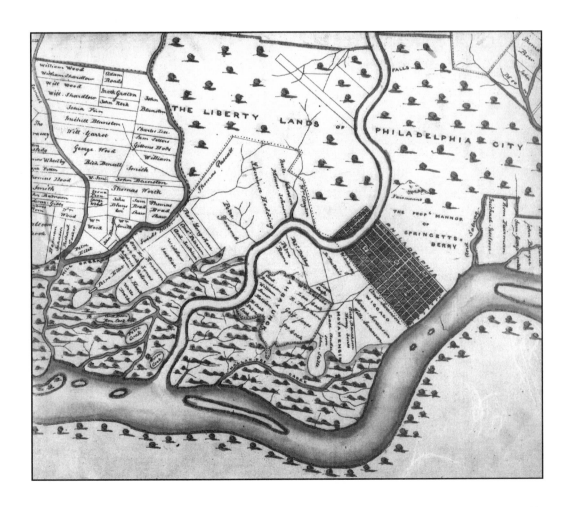

The name of the city came from two Greek words, "philia" (love) and "adelphos" (brother). Today that city is Philadelphia, the City of Brotherly Love.

In 1682, Penn began writing a document outlining the form of government he wanted for his colony. The document, known as the Frame of Government, was very modern for its time. It guaranteed free elections, liberty of conscience, and basic civil rights. Remembering the unjust persecution of Quakers in England, Penn declared that juries in Pennsylvania were to be free of pressure from judges. No one could be imprisoned without being charged with a crime, and murder and treason were the only crimes punishable by death.

Penn also established the governing bodies. Authority was divided into an elected council that proposed legislation and oversaw justice and law enforcement, an elected assembly that could approve or reject the council's laws, and a deputy governor who could act on legislation in Penn's absence.

About 4,000 people had already arrived in the colony when Penn departed for Pennsylvania on August 28, 1682. Guli stayed behind with the children because her mother was ill and needed her care. Two months later, Penn and his fellow Quakers landed at the settlement of New Castle on the Delaware River.

The next day, the *Welcome* sailed north up the Delaware River. In late October, as the party neared Penn's land, the forested hills near the Delaware were blazing with color and the river was thick with migrating ducks.

"Liberty without obedience is confusion, and obedience without liberty is slavery."
—William Penn, in the preface to his Frame of Government

The Frame of Government declared that citizens would "in no way be molested or prejudiced for their religious Persuasion or Practice."

"My dear wife, remember thou wast the love of my youth, and much the joy of my life; the most beloved, as well as the most worthy. . . . God knowest, and thou knowest it, it was a match of Providence's making."
—William to Guli, shortly before his departure for America

In Upland, now known as Chester, Penn was greeted by his cousin, William Markham, whom he had sent to act as deputy governor about six months earlier. Penn set out for Philadelphia almost immediately. At the time of his arrival, fewer than a dozen houses had been built. Following Penn's plan, each house had a large yard, in which settlers could plant gardens and orchards. The wide spaces between houses would prevent the spread of fires like the one that had nearly destroyed London in 1666. For the next two years, Penn lived near the city and oversaw the construction of his house, Pennsbury, on the Delaware River. By 1684, there were nearly 7,000

Pennsbury, Penn's home in Pennsylvania, was surprisingly modest. Penn's dream of spending a quiet life there was not to be.

In this fanciful portrait of Cecil Calvert, the second Lord Baltimore, William Penn is depicted in the wide-brimmed hat, looking over the shoulder of the Maryland proprietor. The third Lord Baltimore (1637-1715), Cecil's son, had a lengthy dispute with Penn over the "Three Lower Counties" of Pennsylvania. These counties would later become the state of Delaware.

colonists from several European countries in Pennsylvania, 2,000 of them in Philadelphia.

Penn was a busy man. He visited New York, New Jersey, and Baltimore, and he explored some of the interior of Pennsylvania. But events in England soon called him back. A baby girl born to Guli six months after Penn sailed for America died, and Guli herself was desperately ill. In addition, Penn faced a land dispute. When the British government had drawn up grants for Penn and for George Calvert, the first Lord Baltimore, no clear borders had been determined between Pennsylvania and Maryland. In the middle of 1684, Charles Calvert, the third Lord Baltimore, sailed for England to argue his case. Penn followed him.

While Penn and Calvert were arguing in the courts in 1685, Charles II died, and his brother was crowned King James II. That was good news for Penn because James II was a friend of his. Penn was even able to convince the king to release 1,300 Quakers from prison. Then, in 1688, James II lost the throne in a bloodless revolution just before signing over the Three Lower Counties to Pennsylvania. William III and his wife Mary II became England's joint rulers. Penn's friendship with James II now made his loyalty to the new rulers suspect, and charges of treason were leveled against him.

After being arrested and released, Penn went into hiding. But even as he suffered this indignity, his mind was still on Pennsylvania. Non-Quakers were pouring into the colony and the government was unstable. Twelve deputy governors served in

Pennsylvania's first eight years as the assembly rebelled against their rule. Penn was also concerned about how much money he was spending on the fledgling colony. Then, due to his political problems in England, Penn lost the proprietorship of his colony early in 1691.

On top of these blows, Guli was very ill again. For eight months, William spent almost every moment by her side. Finally, on February 23, 1694, Guli called William and the children into her room. After gazing on the children lovingly, she sent them away. William remained with her. Three hours later, servants entered the room to find William cradling Guli's head against his chest. She was dead.

For a time after Guli's death, Penn himself was very ill. But with the coming of summer, he gained strength. He was well by August 1694, when King William III gave Pennsylvania back to him. Before returning to America, however, Penn wanted to find a wife and mother for his children. He found her in Hannah Callowhill, a 32-year-old woman from Bristol, England. On March 5, 1696, two years after Guli's death, William and Hannah married.

Penn finally returned to Pennsylvania with Hannah and Letitia in 1699. Eighteen-year-old Billy remained in England. (Penn's oldest son, Springett, had died in 1696.)

Much had changed in the province when Penn and his family arrived in Philadelphia in early December. Fifteen years earlier, the governor had left behind a struggling town. Now he returned to a prosperous settlement. Philadelphia had more than

King William III (1650-1702) was married to his cousin Mary, daughter of King James II. Both he and his wife were grandchildren of King Charles I.

doubled in size, to about 5,000 residents. Many lived in three-story brick homes. Trade and industry flourished.

Penn met with Indian leaders to renew old friendships. To ensure a well-educated populace, he drafted laws calling for schools and compulsory education for both girls and boys up to the age of 12. Penn also ushered through legislation to control smuggling and piracy off Pennsylvania's shoreline.

If William Penn thought his proprietorship of Pennsylvania was now secure, he was in for a surprise. In 1701 the English Parliament grew fearful of Spanish influence in the New World and proposed making all proprietary colonies (like Pennsylvania) the property of the king to shield them from Spain. Late that year, Penn returned to England to protect his interests. Hannah, Letitia, and his American-born son, John, returned to England with him.

The next eight years were difficult for Penn. He was embroiled in legal disputes in England and with some of the Pennsylvania colonists. The establishment of the colony had cost Penn much more money than he ever earned from it. Now broke, Penn even spent time in prison for debt. In addition, he was embarrassed by the actions of his son Billy, who had gone to America and was carousing, gambling, and street-brawling in Philadelphia.

On the evening of October 13, 1712, Penn was writing a long letter to a friend about the possible sale of Pennsylvania to the Crown. The writing stopped in mid-sentence on the fifth page, and a line of ink ran off the page. The founder of Pennsylvania had suffered a stroke. Although he rallied briefly, he had a second stroke four months later. Penn was no longer able to write or to speak in public. For five years he lived as an invalid, his mental capacity destroyed. Sometime in the early morning hours of July 30, 1718, William Penn died at the age of 73. He was buried next to Guli in the family cemetery in England.

After his death, the Indians Penn befriended and protected during his years in Pennsylvania paid him a special tribute. They sent Hannah a gift of furs to wear as a warm cloak as she traveled through the wilderness without her guide.

In the colony of Pennsylvania, William Penn laid the first foundations for a form of government that served the needs of the people being governed. The plan of government he devised was later used as a model for the Constitution of the United States. Thomas Jefferson would call him the "greatest law-giver" the world had ever produced.

After Penn's death, an English Quaker praised him as "a man, a scholar, a friend, a minister, . . . [a man] of extraordinary greatness of mind, free of the stain of ambition."

Quakers and Slavery

Believing as they did in the equality of all human beings, Quakers were the first Europeans to question the institution of slavery. Yet William Penn and many other Quakers in early Pennsylvania and other colonies actually owned slaves. In addition, Quakers living in Rhode Island gained wealth in the slave trade, and Quakers actively and successfully sought to convert to their religion slaveholders in the British colony of Barbados.

Although Quakers would continue to hold slaves up through the Revolutionary War and beyond, in 1688 a group of

Quakers in Germantown, Pennsylvania, made the first public declaration that slavery was wrong because the slaves' natural right to freedom was stolen from them. But this protest was quickly hushed up by people not ready to believe that their practices were sinful.

Quaker opposition to slavery, however, grew in England and the American colonies in the eighteenth century. Some Quaker leaders even began to see slavery as one of the most evil sins. Finally, after more than a half century of protest within Quaker groups, Quaker organizations began to punish members for buying or selling slaves, first in England in 1758 and then in New England in 1760. By the end of the 1760s, most American Quaker slaveowners had pledged to free their slaves.

Quaker Benjamin Franklin helped shape the government of the United States after the Revolutionary War. He opposed slavery and published the first economic argument against its use in 1756.

Quakers and other antislavery activists were horrified by the brutality of slavery. Pictures like this emphasized the cruelty to women and children.

Indentured Servitude

For centuries in England, land had been in short supply and the landless population had grown. Desperately poor, without the means to raise their own food or any place where they could build their own shelter, these landless people could be easily exploited as cheap labor.

The New World changed all this. There were not enough people to work the abundant land in North America. Only the Massachusetts Bay Colony and its offshoots were free of major labor shortages because they were settled by families who needed only to produce enough to sustain life in their colonies. Other colonies—whether controlled by companies, as were Plymouth and New Netherland, or by proprietors, as in Pennsylvania and early Maine, New Hampshire, and New Jersey—had to try to find ways to attract new settlers for labor.

Several colonies tried to enslave the area Indians, but they were not very successful. Many Indians succumbed to European diseases, and survivors easily escaped into the woods. Enslaving Indians also brought the risk of retribution. Then Pennsylvania and other colonies began to import African slaves. Although African slavery was never as important in the Northeast as in the South, Pennsylvania in particular was dependent on slave labor until the American Revolution.

But the Northeast, like the South, relied mostly on a new kind of labor in the seventeenth century: indentured servitude. In exchange for transportation, poor men and women from England came with contracts that gave their labor to a master for a period of servitude, usually five or seven years. Because ship captains were paid according to the number of servants they brought, sometimes people were kidnapped or drugged and forced to sign the contracts of servitude. Other times, convicted criminals were given the option of servitude or execution—often for crimes as minor as pickpocketing or hunting on someone else's land.

For the duration of the period of servitude, these servants were essentially owned by their masters. They were expected to follow orders and could be whipped for disobedience or for running away. Often they were not allowed to marry, and women could be punished for becoming pregnant.

Once their contracts were up, however, the indentured servants were free. Usually contracts stipulated that former servants receive a plot of land, equipment to work it, and clothing. Unlike slaves, who were forced to work for their entire lives with no reward, indentured servants could hope to—and often did—become independent farmers and citizens.

Pennsylvania: From Settlements to Statehood

Philadelphia in 1799, more than a century after Thomas Holme planned the city

Although William Penn was rarely in the colony he founded, his influence continued to be felt there for many years after his death. The friendly relations he had established with the Indian tribes living in or near the colony helped to maintain peace for many years.

By 1750, however, the growth of the colony's population and the need for additional land was straining relations between colonists and the Indians. The situation grew worse when British traders and settlers streamed into western Pennsylvania, hungry for land. Eager to protect their fur trade, the French joined forces with the Native Americans to drive out the English. The result was the French and Indian War, which erupted in 1754. When this war finally ended in 1763 with the defeat of the French and their Indian allies, the expansion of Pennsylvania resumed.

With the beginning of the American Revolution in April 1775, Pennsylvania quickly took center stage. Men from Pennsylvania served as soldiers in many of the important battles of the war, and the colony formed its own navy to defend its shores. Many major battles were fought on Pennsylvania's soil.

The colony was also a center for political activity during the war years. The First Continental Congress met in Philadelphia, and the Declaration of Independence was also signed in the City of Brotherly Love when the Second Continental Congress gathered there. In 1787, delegates to the Constitutional Convention in Philadelphia wrote the United States Constitution. On December 12, 1787, Pennsylvania became the second state to join the union.

The signing of the Declaration of Independence in Independence Hall in Philadelphia, 1776

A Northeastern Timeline

1497 and 1498: John Cabot and his son Sebastian sail along the East Coast and claim North America for England.

1511: Portuguese explorer Miguel Corte Real probably approaches the Rhode Island coast by water.

1524: Giovanni da Verrazano, an Italian explorer, sails the New England coast seeking a waterway through the continent.

1536: King Henry VIII of England establishes the Anglican Church (Church of England).

July 1586: **Thomas Hooker** is born in Leicestershire, England.

January 12, 1588: **John Winthrop** is born in Suffolk, England.

March 1590: **William Bradford** is born in Austerfield, England.

July 1591: **Anne Hutchinson** is born in Lincolnshire, England.

c. 1592: **John Wheelwright** is born in Lincolnshire, England.

1602: Englishman Bartholomew Gosnold explores Massachusetts's coastal region, naming Cape Cod and Martha's Vineyard.

c. 1603: **Roger Williams** is born in London, England.

1603: Englishman Martin Pring sails up the Piscataqua River between Maine and New Hampshire.

1604: Frenchman Samuel de Champlain tries to found a settlement in Maine.

1608: **Bradford** and other Separatists flee England for Leiden, Holland, to escape persecution by the Church of England.

1609: Sailing for the Dutch East India Company, Henry Hudson heads up the Hudson River in New York.

July 4, 1609: Samuel de Champlain is the first European to see Vermont.

1610: **Peter Stuyvesant** is born in the town of Friesland in the Netherlands.

1613: The Dutch establish several settlements in New Netherland.

1614: John Smith explores the coast north of Virginia and names it New England.

1614: Adriaen Block, a Dutch explorer, discovers the Connecticut River and claims Connecticut for the Netherlands.

1614: The Dutch explore the Delaware River and claim what will be Pennsylvania.

1619: The first Africans arrive in North America as servants.

1620: King James I grants a charter for New England to the Council for New England.

November 11, 1620: The Pilgrims sign the Mayflower Compact with their non-Pilgrim companions.

December 11, 1620: **Bradford** and the Pilgrims land at Plymouth in what is now Massachusetts.

April 1621: When John Carver dies, **Bradford** is elected governor of Plymouth.

1621: The Council for New England grants land to Plymouth Colony.

1621: The Dutch West India Company is established to manage Dutch claims in the New World, Australia, and West Africa.

Autumn 1621: The Plymouth settlers and the Wampanoag Indians celebrate the first Thanksgiving.

1622: Sir Ferdinando Gorges and John Mason are granted the province of Maine, a region including present-day New Hampshire and Maine.

1624: The Dutch West India Company builds Fort Orange near what is now Albany, New York.

1626: Peter Minuit buys Manhattan Island for the Dutch West India Company for the equivalent of $24.

1627: **Bradford** and seven other Pilgrims pay off the debt on Plymouth to maintain local ownership and control.

1628: William Laud, a sworn enemy of Puritans and other "nonconformists" who refuse to obey Anglican Church policies, becomes bishop of London.

1628: The New England Company starts a Puritan colony in Salem, Massachusetts, under the governorship of John Endecott.

March 4, 1629: The Massachusetts Bay Company (formerly the New England Company) receives a charter for the Massachusetts Bay Colony.

1629: Sir Ferdinando Gorges and John Mason split their Maine grant into Maine, which Gorges takes, and New Hampshire, which is retained by Mason.

Summer 1629: **Winthrop** is elected governor of the Massachusetts Bay Colony.

June 1630: **Winthrop** and the Puritans arrive in the Massachusetts Bay Colony.

February 1631: **Williams** lands in the Massachusetts Bay Colony.

1632: In England, Bishop William Laud orders **Wheelwright** to stop preaching.

1633: William Laud becomes archbishop of Canterbury and steps up persecution of Puritans and other nonconformists.

Spring 1633: Fleeing arrest by Laud in England, **Hooker** comes to Massachusetts.

1633: The Dutch establish the House of Good Hope on the Connecticut River, laying claim to the Connecticut region.

1633: Trader John Oldham opens a trail from Boston to Connecticut.

1634: Massachusetts claims Connecticut as its territory.

September 1634: **Hutchinson** lands in Boston, Massachusetts.

1635: **Hutchinson** begins holding religious meetings in her home.

October 1635: **Williams** is sentenced to banishment from Massachusetts.

October 1635: Some of the members of **Hooker**'s congregation make their way to Hartford in the Connecticut territory.

Spring 1636: **Williams** purchases land and settles Providence, Rhode Island.

May 1636: **Hooker** leads the rest of his congregation to Connecticut.

May 26, 1636: **Wheelwright** arrives in Boston, Massachusetts.

1636-1637: In the Pequot War, English settlers in New England wipe out the Pequot Indians after several years of skirmishes and violence.

November 1637: Wheelwright is banished from the Massachusetts Bay Colony by the General Court.

November 1637: Hutchinson appears before the General Court and is banished from the Massachusetts Bay Colony.

1638: John Davenport and Theophilus Eaton found the theocracy of New Haven.

March 1638: Minuit establishes New Sweden on the Delaware River in present-day Delaware.

March 22, 1638: Hutchinson is excommunicated from the Boston church.

April 1638: After reaching Rhode Island, **Hutchinson** founds the settlement of Portsmouth.

April 1638: Wheelwright buys land for Exeter, New Hampshire, from the Indians.

January 1639: Hartford, Windsor, and Wethersfield unite as Connecticut Colony.

1639: William Coddington leaves the town of Portsmouth and founds a settlement at Newport, Rhode Island.

1640: Bradford and the other holders of the charter to Plymouth Colony turn the colony over to the settlers.

1641: The Body of Liberties is passed as the first set of laws in the Massachusetts Bay Colony; it includes the first statute permitting slavery in North America.

1642: Hutchinson moves her family to Long Island in today's New York when the Massachusetts Bay Colony threatens to take over Rhode Island.

1642-1648: In the English Civil War, Puritans fight King Charles I for the right to have a powerful Parliament.

1643: Samuel Gorton leaves Providence and founds Warwick, Rhode Island.

1643: New Sweden spreads into what is now Chester, Pennsylvania.

1643: The Massachusetts Bay Colony, Plymouth, New Haven, and Connecticut form the Confederation of New England.

1643: After Massachusetts makes claim to New Hampshire as part of its territory, **Wheelwright** moves to Maine.

August or September 1643: Hutchinson and her family are murdered by Indians.

May 1644: Massachusetts lifts the order of banishment from **Wheelwright**.

1644: Williams receives a patent from England uniting Providence, Portsmouth, Newport, and Warwick as Providence Plantations (later called Rhode Island).

October 14, 1644: William Penn is born in London, England.

Summer 1646: Stuyvesant is appointed governor of New Netherland.

1647: George Fox founds the Society of Friends of the Truth, soon called Quakers.

May 11, 1647: Stuyvesant lands in New Amsterdam, New Netherland.

Spring 1647: Wheelwright returns to the Massachusetts Bay Colony, taking a position as a minister in Hampton in what is now New Hampshire.

July 7, 1647: Hooker dies at age 61.

1649: The Puritan Commonwealth government takes power in England.

January 1649: King Charles I is beheaded by the Puritans who defeated him in the English Civil War.

Spring 1649: Winthrop dies at age 61.

1651: Coddington convinces the English to split Rhode Island into two parts and make him governor of Aquidneck Island.

1652: Coddington's commission to govern half of Rhode Island is rescinded.

1652: The Massachusetts Bay Colony claims the territory of Maine.

1654: Oliver Cromwell becomes lord protector of England with a constitution that gives him dictatorial powers in the Puritan government in England.

1655: **Stuyvesant** defeats the Swedish colony of New Sweden.

May 9, 1657: **Bradford** dies at age 67.

1660: King Charles II is restored to the English throne, overthrowing the Puritan Commonwealth government.

1662: Winthrop's son John Winthrop Jr., the governor of Connecticut, obtains a charter for Connecticut from the king.

1663: King Charles II gives a new charter to Rhode Island.

1664: King Charles II makes a grant of New Netherland, which he considers English territory, to his brother James, the duke of York, and renames it New York.

September 1664: **Stuyvesant** surrenders New Netherland to the English.

1664: New Jersey is separated from New York and becomes a proprietary colony under George Carteret and John Berkeley.

January 1665: New Haven becomes part of Connecticut.

July 1667: **Penn** becomes a Quaker and is soon arrested for his beliefs.

1672: **Stuyvesant** dies at age 62.

1674: A group of Quakers purchases West Jersey (western New Jersey) from proprietor John Berkeley to start a colony.

1675-1676: Metacomet (or King Philip) leads the Wampanoag and Narragansett Indians in King Philip's War. The bloody and destructive fight between the Indians and the colonists ended in complete victory for the English.

1677: Massachusetts buys Maine from the proprietor's heirs.

November 15, 1679: **Wheelwright** dies at age 87.

1681: **Penn** and other Quaker leaders buy George Carteret's East Jersey in the hope of founding a Quaker colony.

March 4, 1681: King James II grants the colony of Pennsylvania to **Penn**.

1682: **Penn** writes Pennsylvania's Frame of Government, guaranteeing religious liberty, free elections, and basic civil rights.

October 1682: **Penn** and the Quakers come to his Pennsylvania colony.

Early 1683: **Williams** dies at the age of about 80.

1684: King James II revokes the charter of the Massachusetts Bay Colony.

1686: Sir Edmund Andros becomes governor of the Dominion of New England.

1688: New York and New Jersey are added to the Dominion of New England.

1688: The Glorious Revolution drives King James II from the throne of England.

1688: Sir Edmund Andros loses power in America when King James II is deposed.

1689-1691: Jacob Leisler rules New York after its rebellion against England.

1691: **Penn** loses control of Pennsylvania.

March 1691: The English government retakes control of New York.

1691: The Massachusetts Bay Colony receives a charter making Plymouth and Maine part of Massachusetts.

August 1694: **Penn** regains possession of his colony.

1701: Pennsylvania again becomes a royal colony.

1702: New Jersey's proprietors turn the colony over to the English Crown.

July 30, 1718: **Penn** dies at age 73.

1724: Fort Dummer, near Brattleboro, is Vermont's first European settlement.

1741: England grants New Hampshire land that includes present-day Vermont.

1754-1763: The French and Indian War rages between the French, their Indian allies, and the British until the British win control of Canada and the interior of what becomes the United States.

1764: New Hampshire loses the New Hampshire Grants to New York.

1765: The British Parliament passes the Stamp Act, taxing American colonists; furor over taxation without representation leads ultimately to the Revolutionary War.

1770: In the Boston Massacre, British soldiers fire on colonists resisting taxation.

1773: Massachusetts colonists at what we call the Boston Tea Party destroy tea that the British government is taxing.

April 19, 1775: The Battles of Lexington and Concord start the Revolutionary War.

July 4, 1776: The American colonies declare their independence from England.

July 1777: The Green Mountain Boys establish an independent republic in what will be Vermont.

September 3, 1783: The Treaty of Paris formally ends the Revolutionary War.

1787: The U.S. Constitution is written by the delegates to the Constitutional Convention in Philadelphia.

December 12, 1787: Pennsylvania becomes the new nation's second state. Its capital has been Harrisburg since 1812.

December 18, 1787: New Jersey joins the United States as the third state. Trenton becomes its capital in 1790.

January 9, 1788: Connecticut is the United States' fifth state. Its capital is Hartford.

February 6, 1788: Massachusetts enters the United States as the sixth state, with Boston as its capital.

June 21, 1788: New Hampshire becomes the ninth state in the nation. Concord is named its capital in 1808.

July 26, 1788: New York becomes the eleventh state in the United States. Albany becomes New York's capital in 1797.

May 29, 1790: Rhode Island joins the nation as the thirteenth state. Newport and Providence are joint capitals until 1900, when Providence becomes the sole capital.

March 4, 1791: Vermont is the fourteenth state to join the United States. Montpelier has been its capital since 1805.

March 15, 1820: Maine separates from Massachusetts and becomes the nation's 23rd state. Augusta is named the state capital in 1831.

Source Notes

Quoted passages are noted by page and order of citation. Spelling and some capitalizations are modernized.

Introduction

p. 10 (margin): Giles Gunn, ed., *Early American Writing* (New York: Penguin, 1994), 98.

Chapter One

p. 16: William Bradford, *Of Plymouth Plantation*, ed. by Samuel Eliot Morison (New York: Knopf, 1952), 59-60.

p. 17: Bradford, *Of Plymouth Plantation*, 75-76.

p. 18: Bradford, *Of Plymouth Plantation*, 72.

p. 21 (margin): Bradford, *Of Plymouth Plantation*, 95.

p. 21: Bradford, *Of Plymouth Plantation*, 81.

p. 22 (first): Bradford, *Of Plymouth Plantation*, 90.

p. 22 (second): Bradford, *Of Plymouth Plantation*, 92.

p. 23 (both): Bradford, *Of Plymouth Plantation*, 110.

p. 27 (margin): Bradford, *Of Plymouth Plantation*, 253.

p. 27: Francis Murphy, introduction to *Of Plymouth Plantation*, by William Bradford (New York: Random House, 1981), xvi.

Chapter Two

p. 29: David Hawke, *The Colonial Experience* (New York: Macmillan, 1966), 133-134.

p. 31 (margin): Samuel Eliot Morison, *Builders of the Bay Colony* (Boston: Northeastern University Press, 1981), 64.

p. 33: Morison, *Builders*, 60-61.

p. 34 (margin): James G. Moseley, *John Winthrop's World: History as a Story; the Story as History* (Madison: University of Wisconsin Press, 1992), 39.

p. 34: Moseley, *John Winthrop's World*, 42.

p. 35 (margin): Moseley, *John Winthrop's World*, 48.

p. 37 (margin): Edmund S. Morgan, *The Puritan Dilemma: The Story of John Winthrop* (Boston: Little, Brown, 1958), 105-106.

p. 41: Morgan, *The Puritan Dilemma*, 154.

p. 43: Moseley, *John Winthrop's World*, 28.

Chapter Three

p. 47: J. Franklin Jameson, ed., *Narratives of New Netherland* (New York: Barnes & Noble, 1953), 342.

p. 51: Henri van der Zee and Barbara van der Zee, *A Sweet and Alien Land: The Story of Dutch New York* (New York: Viking, 1978), 159.

p. 53 (margin): van der Zee, *A Sweet and Alien Land*, 164.

p. 54 (margin): Jameson, *Narratives*, 330.

pp. 54-55: van der Zee, *A Sweet and Alien Land*, 184.

p. 55 (first margin): Jameson, *Narratives*, 337.

p. 55 (second margin): van der Zee, *A Sweet and Alien Land*, 165.

Chapter Four

p. 70 (first margin): Ola Elizabeth Winslow, *Master Roger Williams: A Biography* (New York: Macmillan, 1957), 35.

p. 70 (second margin): Winslow, *Master Roger Williams*, 46.

p. 72 (margin): Bradford, *Of Plymouth Plantation*, 257.

p. 73 (margin): Winslow, *Master Roger Williams*, 119.

p. 73 (all): Winslow, *Master Roger Williams*, 125-126.

p. 74 (caption): Winslow, *Master Roger Williams*, 127, 103.

p. 77 (margin): Paul Angle, ed., *By These Words: Great Documents of American Liberty* (New York: Rand McNally, 1954), 12-13.

p. 80 (margin): Winslow, *Master Roger Williams*, 216.

p. 83: Edmund S. Morgan, *Roger Williams: The Church and the State* (New York: Norton, 1967), 46.

Chapter Five

p. 92 (caption): Selma R. Williams, *Divine Rebel: The Life of Anne Marbury Hutchinson* (New York: Holt, Rinehart and Winston, 1981), 98.

p. 92: Williams, *Divine Rebel*, 115.

p. 93 (margin): Williams, *Divine Rebel*, 97.

p. 94 (margin): David Hawke, ed., *U.S. Colonial History: Readings and Documents* (New York: Bobbs-Merrill, 1966), 116.

p. 94 (first): Williams, *Divine Rebel*, 133.

p. 94 (second): Williams, *Divine Rebel*, 161.

p. 95 (margin): Williams, *Divine Rebel*, 97-98.

p. 95 (first): Williams, *Divine Rebel*, 161.

p. 95 (second, third, fourth): Williams, *Divine Rebel*, 166.

p. 96 (first): Deborah Crawford, *Four Women in a Violent Time* (New York: Crown, 1970), 133.

p. 96 (second): Williams, *Divine Rebel*, 187.

p. 97 (margin): Williams, *Divine Rebel*, 96-97.

p. 97: Williams, *Divine Rebel*, 192-193.

p. 98: Crawford, *Four Women*, 169.

p. 100 (margin): John Heard Jr., *John Wheelwright, 1592-1679* (Boston: Houghton Mifflin, 1930), 90.

Chapter Six

p. 104: Frank Shuffelton, *Thomas Hooker, 1586-1647* (Princeton, N.J.: Princeton University Press, 1977), 159.

p. 105 (margin): Leland Ryken, *Worldly Saints* (Grand Rapids, Mich.: Zondervan, 1986), 40.

p. 106: Shuffelton, *Thomas Hooker*, 128.

p. 107 (margin): Dumas Malone, ed., *Dictionary of American Biography* (New York: Scribner's, 1936), 199.

p. 108 (margin): Shuffelton, *Thomas Hooker*, 164.

p. 108 (caption): Shuffelton, *Thomas Hooker*, 76.

pp. 108-109: Shuffelton, *Thomas Hooker*, 197.

p. 112 (margin): Shuffelton, *Thomas Hooker*, 236.

p. 113 (all): Malone, *Dictionary of American Biography*, 200.

p. 114: Shuffelton, *Thomas Hooker*, 279.

Chapter Seven

p. 119: Heard Jr., *John Wheelwright*, 10.

p. 123: Heard Jr., *John Wheelwright*, 42.

p. 124 (margin): Moseley, *John Winthrop's World*, 82.

p. 124: Malone, *Dictionary of American Biography*, 62.

p. 126 (margin): Heard Jr., *John Wheelwright*, 60.

p. 126: Gunn, *Early American Writing*, 99.

p. 128: Heard Jr., *John Wheelwright*, 67.

p. 130: Heard Jr., *John Wheelwright*, 85-86.

p. 131: Heard Jr., *John Wheelwright*, 86.

p. 132 (margin): Heard Jr., *John Wheelwright*, 12.

Chapter Eight

p. 140: George Fox, *The Journal of George Fox* (New York: Dutton, 1962), 34.

p. 142 (first): Hanz Fantel, *William Penn: Apostle of Dissent* (New York: Morrow, 1974), 60.

p. 142 (second): Harry Emerson Wildes, *William Penn* (New York: Macmillan, 1974), 45.

p. 143: Wildes, *William Penn*, 52.

p. 144 (margin): Fantel, *William Penn*, 91.

p. 144: Fantel, *William Penn*, 126.

p. 145: Sydney George Fisher, *The True William Penn* (Philadelphia: Lippincott, 1900), 146.

p. 146 (margin): Hildegarde Dolson, *William Penn: Quaker Hero* (New York: Random House, 1971), 100.

p. 148 (first and second margin): Dolson, *William Penn*, 104.

p. 148 (third margin): Fantel, *William Penn*, 161.

p. 153 (margin): Dolson, *William Penn*, 180.

p. 153: William Hull, *William Penn: A Topical Biography* (London: Oxford University Press, 1937), 336.

Bibliography

Andrews, Charles M. *The Colonial Period of American History.* Vol. 1. New Haven, Conn.: Yale University Press, 1964.

Angle, Paul, ed. *By These Words: Great Documents of American Liberty.* New York: Rand McNally, 1954.

Boorstin, Daniel J. *The Americans: The Colonial Experience.* New York: Random House, 1958.

Bradford, William. *Of Plymouth Plantation.* Edited by Samuel Eliot Morison. New York: Knopf, 1952.

Brandon, William. *Indians.* Boston: Houghton Mifflin, 1987.

Chupack, Henry. *Roger Williams.* New York: Twayne, 1969.

Crawford, Deborah. *Four Women in a Violent Time.* New York: Crown, 1970.

Davis, David Brion. *The Problem of Slavery in Western Culture.* New York: Oxford University Press, 1966.

Deetz, James. *In Small Things Forgotten: An Archaeology of Early American Life.* New York: Anchor, 1996.

Dolson, Hildegarde. *William Penn: Quaker Hero.* New York: Random House, 1971.

Dow, George Francis. *Every Day Life in the Massachusetts Bay Colony.* New York: Dover, 1988.

Fantel, Hanz. *William Penn: Apostle of Dissent.* New York: Morrow, 1974.

Ferris, Robert, ed. *Explorers and Settlers: Historic Places Commemorating the Early Exploration and Settlement of the United States.* Washington, D.C.: U.S. Department of the Interior, 1968.

Fisher, Sydney George. *The True William Penn.* Philadelphia: Lippincott, 1900.

Fox, George. *The Journal of George Fox.* New York: Dutton, 1962.

Goetzmann, William H., and Glyndwr Williams. *The Atlas of North American Exploration: From the Norse Voyages to the Race to the Pole*. New York: Prentice Hall, 1992.

Gray, Robert. *A History of London*. New York: Taplinger, 1979.

Gunn, Giles, ed. *Early American Writing*. New York: Penguin, 1994.

Hawke, David. *The Colonial Experience*. New York: Macmillan, 1966.

———, ed. *Everyday Life in Early America*. New York: Harper & Row, 1988.

———, ed. *U.S. Colonial History: Readings and Documents*. New York: Bobbs-Merrill, 1966.

Heard, John, Jr. *John Wheelwright, 1592-1679*. Boston: Houghton Mifflin, 1930.

Hodge, Frederick Webb, ed. *Handbook of American Indians North of Mexico*. 2 vols. Totowa, N.J.: Rowman and Littlefield, 1975.

Hull, William. *William Penn: A Topical Biography*. London: Oxford University Press, 1937.

Jameson, J. Franklin, ed. *Narratives of New Netherland, 1609-1664*. New York: Barnes & Noble, 1953.

Kehoe, Alice Beck. *North American Indians: A Comprehensive Account*. Englewood Cliffs, N.J.: Prentice Hall, 1992.

Kessler, Henry Howard, and Eugene Rachlis. *Peter Stuyvesant and His New York*. New York: Random House, 1959.

Loewen, James W. *Lies My Teacher Told Me: Everything Your American History Textbook Got Wrong*. New York: Simon & Schuster, 1995.

Morgan, Edmund S. *The Puritan Dilemma: The Story of John Winthrop*. Boston: Little, Brown, 1958.

———. *Roger Williams: The Church and the State*. New York: Norton, 1967.

Morgan, Ted. *Wilderness at Dawn: The Settling of the North American Continent*. New York: Simon & Schuster, 1993.

Morison, Samuel Eliot. *Builders of the Bay Colony*. Boston: Northeastern University Press, 1981.

Morrill, John, ed. *The Oxford Illustrated History of Tudor and Stuart Britain*. Oxford: Oxford University Press, 1996.

Moseley, James G. *John Winthrop's World: History as a Story; the Story as History*. Madison: University of Wisconsin Press, 1992.

Murphy, Francis. Introduction to *Of Plymouth Plantation*, by William Bradford. New York: Random House, 1981.

Porter, Roy. *London: A Social History*. London: Hamish Hamilton, 1994.

Ryken, Leland. *Worldly Saints*. Grand Rapids, Mich.: Zondervan, 1986.

Shuffelton, Frank. *Thomas Hooker, 1586-1647*. Princeton, N.J.: Princeton University Press, 1977.

Smith, Bradford. *Bradford of Plymouth*. Philadelphia: Lippincott, 1951.

Snell, Tee Loftin. *The Wild Shores: America's Beginnings*. Washington, D.C.: National Geographic Society, 1974.

van der Zee, Henri, and Barbara van der Zee. *A Sweet and Alien Land: The Story of Dutch New York*. New York: Viking, 1978.

Vaughan, Alden. *New England Frontier: Puritan and Indians, 1620-1675*. Boston: Little, Brown, 1965.

Ward, Harry M. *Colonial America, 1607-1763*. Englewood Cliffs, N.J.: Prentice Hall, 1991.

Westbrook, Perry D. *William Bradford*. Boston: Twayne, 1978.

Wildes, Harry Emerson. *William Penn*. New York: Macmillan, 1974.

Williams, Selma R. *Divine Rebel: The Life of Anne Marbury Hutchinson*. New York: Holt, Rinehart and Winston, 1981.

Winslow, Ola Elizabeth. *Master Roger Williams: A Biography*. New York: Macmillan, 1957.

Zinn, Howard. *A People's History of the United States*. New York: HarperCollins, 1990.

Index

About the Author

Kieran Doherty is a longtime journalist and business writer as well as a nonfiction writer for young adults. He has written young-adult biographies about William Penn and William Bradford. In the **Shaping America** series, Doherty is the author of *Soldiers, Cavaliers, and Planters: Settlers of the Southeastern Colonies*; *Explorers, Missionaries, and Trappers: Trailblazers of the West*; and *Ranchers, Homesteaders, and Traders: Frontiersmen of the South-Central States*. An avid sailor, he lives in Boynton Beach, Florida, with his wife, Lynne.

Photo Credits